Praise for **The Unapologetic Woman**

Dr. Danita Johnson Woods has done it again with her new powerful book *The Unapologetic Woman: Leading with Power and Confidence*. I purchased it for my wife, my sister and my daughter because I thought it was a must read for them. As I read it, I realized that I could gain a lot from it as well. Buy the book and read it. It will help you avoid lots of common mistakes in your career.

—Mike LaBroi, CIO, Edgewater Health

Dr. Danita Johnson Woods delivers powerful words of wisdom. *The Unapologetic Woman* is enticing to say the least! A great read with chapters of inspiring tales of our challenges and "opportunities" to shine as woman leaders. You will find yourself smiling and acknowledging the truthfulness and introspective reflection of how powerful and confident women can and should be. Her book is an inspiration for all women seeking to be leaders or already in leadership roles.

—Janice L. Ryba, CEO & Administrator, St. Mary Medical Center

Danita Johnson Woods' powerful combination of tough love and straight talk make *The Unapologetic Woman* a must-read for both men and women.

—Nick Morgan, author of *Power Cues: The Subtle Science of Leading Groups, Persuading Others, and Maximizing Your Personal Impact*

Dr. Johnson Woods is "spot-on" that women make fantastic leaders if they stop the rhetoric of apology. The author not only identifies the problem but offers concrete solutions.

—Amazon Customer

I truly enjoyed *The Unapologetic Woman: Leading with Power and Confidence.* Dr. Wood's straight talk mixed with personal experience helped me to understand and overcome barriers associated with fearing success! The chapters are creative but substantive. It is a quick and worthy read.   **—LaTanya W.**

I would recommend this book for anyone who wants to improve herself. Easy to read, I will keep this book as a reference on my bookshelf for further inspiration when I need it.

—Theresa Jameson

Throughout this book, Dr. Johnson Woods' words were very powerful. It had a great impact on me knowing that there is nothing I can't do if I put my mind to it. I walked away with a sense of purpose and taking on the world.   **—Bridget Cheatham**

I appreciate the open and honest dialogue. As a professional woman, I find that we are always apologizing, sometimes unconsciously to our colleagues, staff and leaders for speaking up or for having an opinion. The book opened my eyes and taught me to accept my decisions without apologizing for them!   **—Arlene Mitchell-Pace**

Dr. Johnson Woods provides great strategies for dealing with various personal and workplace challenges that often impede a woman's success, especially the "sorry syndrome."

—Amazon Customer

the

Women's

Little Purple Book for Leadership

How to Create Success through **Persuasion, Power** and **Presence**

Dr. Danita Johnson Woods

The Women's Little Purple Book for Leadership
How to Create Success through Persuasion, Power and Presence
Copyright © 2026 by Danita Johnson Woods Enterprises, LLC
All rights reserved.

Published by Vitality Ventures Press
Book Consultant: Judith Briles, The Book Shepherd
Editor: Peggie Ireland
Cover, Interior Design, and eBook conversion:
Rebecca Finkel, F+P Graphic Design

Books may be purchased in quantity by contacting the publisher
or author: DrDanitaJohnsonWoods.com or email:
DrDanitaJ@gmail.com.

Library of Congress Control Number: need
ISBN:
ebook: 978-0-9972124-4-0
Paperback: 979-8-9958258-0-7
Hardcover: 979-8-9958258-1-4
audiobook: 978-0-9972124-5-7

Business | Leadership | Women
Second Edition
Printed in the USA

Books by Dr. Danita Johnson Woods

The Women's Little Purple Book for Leadership

The Unapologetic Woman

Influencing Today's Youth

Power from Within

Contents

Author's Note

I have learned many things in my lifetime. Most have been positive experiences, while some have been hard lessons in reality. But nevertheless, as I look back on them, there were valuable teaching moments that helped me a great deal as well. I think of it as the good, the bad, and sometimes downright ugly.

Many of the things I've learned over the trajectory of my career have left me wondering:

- How did I get here?

- How did my life experiences cause me to land in this place or to occupy this space where I am today?

- How have I grown from these experiences, and could I have avoided some of the pitfalls?

- What will be next?

One of the most important things I've learned is that women bring a unique perspective to leadership … the good, the bad, and sometimes downright ugly. Here's what I know:

- It took me years to develop my personal style …
  and it will take you years as well.

- It took me what seemed like endless time to develop my own skills for relationship building and the collaboration to accomplish my organization's goals.

- It took me time to accomplish my personal goals. And, most likely, you will duplicate the time I spent in developing as a leader and acquiring the skills needed as I did.

To help you on your journey, I want to share some of the things I wish I'd known early in my career—things that will help you along the way.

Remember, good leaders are hard to find—at any level of an organization. My hope is that the pearls contained in this book will help you enjoy a successful leadership path and allow you to stand out as an amazing leader … the leader you were meant to be.

—Danita

1

I Am Woman, Hear Me Roar!

Can I get people to go with me and accept the pain, discomfort, and the "shock of the new" to get to a better place?

The year 2020 has been labeled as UNFORGETTABLE for every leader. To move ahead, to survive, to reach a point where leadership can bring an organization to sustainability, leaders attained levels of flexibility that were not imagined in previous years. Some organizations didn't make it through. Others had to do things differently and fast to survive. In my field of health care, much was unfamiliar and sometimes, downright scary.

Our leadership team was fortunate to see the seriousness of COVID-19 and what its impact could be on our facilities, our patients, and us. Almost overnight, 90% of my staff was working from home. As the ultimate decision maker, I made sure that all staff had the equipment they needed—from computers, to extra phone lines, to mobile phones, to tech training and assistance—and paid for it. Then there were the patients … many needed tech training assistance so that they could communicate with the organization as well as with the doctors who were providing care.

Infection control procedures were revamped overnight: more frequent cleaning; masks for everyone; temperature checks on everyone entering the buildings; and isolation rooms set up in case someone was identified as ill. Most meetings were virtual. Very few got sick.

Leading is not easy. Good leaders are rare and great ones … they are worth their weight in gold. Your success or failure as a leader relies on your ability to apply your best-laid plans in what the old Chinese saying identifies as "interesting times." And times are always interesting. My three decades plus have revealed this truth: *Leadership is never simple and never easy.*

Leadership involves convincing people that change is necessary and yet change, even the best kind imaginable, brings with it a certain amount of pain. A good leader can get people to move past the pain and can spur them into action.

Be intentional in your quest to be a great listener so that you can become a great leader.

Great leadership requires you to be more than a good listener … it means being a *great* listener. In fact, it is an essential and valuable skill for anyone in leadership. Actively listening to others is one of the best ways to improve your leadership skills. You can do this by eliminating distractions and "outside" noise. Today's workplaces are woven with electronic gadgets of all sorts—perfect distractors that reduce listening. Listening doesn't mean practicing the art of multitasking. Even worse, are you allowing your mind to fast forward anticipating the next meeting? Are you thinking about what the person who is talking will say next?

Knowing you care about your team members and are interested in what they have to say in the present, helps to create a bond that will improve your working relationship and your individual and team effectiveness and productivity.

Leadership means that goals are clearly defined, set, and effectively communicated.

As a leader, you will spend most of your time communicating with members of your team. So, why not focus on being intentional in your quest to be a great listener so that you can become a great leader? You will be surprised that, in turn, others will tend to listen to you more carefully as a result.

Leadership means that goals are clearly defined, set, and effectively communicated.

Setting reasonable and attainable goals contributes to the success of a team. Successful leaders typically start with a plan that defines what they want to achieve and how they will go about making it happen. It establishes the vision, priorities, and the framework for the organization's strategic direction.

As a leader, how do you:

- Measure the morale of the organization?

- Ascertain the true reputation of the organization?

- Determine the financial health of your organization?

- Clarify your vision to the skeptics?

- Motivate team members?

- Mobilize the resources you have?

- Keep your employees focused?

- Provide benchmarks for measuring progress?

- Spotlight areas for revision?

- Give your team something to strive for?

- Celebrate successes?

For leaders, goal setting is immensely important. Your goal setting takes time and commitment. Do not take any shortcuts; it is a process. Executive teams usually plan a "getaway" of some sort where there are no distractors to disrupt the goal-setting mission. Annually, I take my executive team and the board on a two-day retreat. That "process" delivers a variety of pluses for the team. Here are the takeaways:

1. It solidifies that we are a team.

2. It helps everyone focus on the tasks of the organization.

3. It creates a visual map of where the organization can go.

4. Everyone present contributes.

5. Participants feel that their ownership quotient increases.

Accomplishing the needs of the organization can most effectively happen if you have a clearly defined set of goals to guide you. Your team members can grow in their roles when they clearly understand and are working toward meeting the expectations of the organization.

How can I accomplish more? is a common question most leaders ask … over and over. I would like to say it is simple, but it's not. If you are creating goals that guide their short- and long-range activities, your team members should have a guide map. They benefit by knowing what is expected of them and having a game plan to follow. *Do you?*

Achieving daily and immediate activities become much easier when everyone is striving to meet the same end. *Have you communicated clearly and effectively what that "end" is?* Choose your goals wisely because in the end, you will improve your leadership skills and guide your team to success. Everyone wins.

Can I get the people who work in my company to go with me ... to accept the pain, discomfort, and the "shock of the new" to get to a better place?

—Dr. Danita Johnson Woods

the **Leader's Checklist**

As a leader, you need to know and understand why you have chosen a leadership position. You need to know what your method of leadership is. And does it connect with those you are leading?

They Say You Can't Unscramble Scrambled Eggs ... But You Can.

The Edgewater Health Story

My position was, "You hired me, so trust me, support me, and together we can turn this organization around."

It would be foolish of me to write a book for women on leadership if I personally had not been in the trenches myself. Too many proclaim that they are experts, yet are they really?

Before I transitioned into the Edgewater Health System, I was the CEO of a long-term healthcare system. Prior to that, I was #2 in a mental health system, which I saw as a stepping-stone position. I needed to show that I could lead an organization!

No one told me that I was stepping into a massive loop-de-loop roller coaster of proportions that I would never have believed if someone had attempted to forewarn me.

The Edgewater Story

Truth be told, challenges keep me motivated. My adrenaline flows into overdrive when I knowingly go into poorly functioning organizations or troubled situations. But it doesn't deter me. I eagerly accept the task of turning situations around. And even better, I've succeeded beyond the expectations of those who have hired me … and even myself!

Edgewater Health was the poster child of a horribly run organization … one that was so bad, that few really understood the depth of trouble it was in, including me. As its new Chief Executive Officer, all my grit, skills, and tenacity were needed if I was to right this sinking ship. It was in a state of complete chaos, facing the threat of a revoked operating license, and worse yet … on the brink of bankruptcy. Employee morale was barely breathing; it was more a whimper. Edgewater Health was on the brink of closing its doors forever.

When I became the CEO, the center's annual budget was around $8 million. The organization provided an extensive range of behavioral health programs. Its services included an inpatient unit, outpatient care for children, adolescents, adults, and addiction counseling. There were residential programs for youth and group homes for adults with chronic mental illness. Approximately 160 employees delivered these services. But, and it was a significant BUT, they were poorly and inadequately delivered to a community badly in need of them.

In what seemed like a massive contradiction, the center dealt with two major problems daily.

1. There was a very long list of people waiting to get into a service.

2. The normal referral sources such as the courts and the Office of Family and Children Services were concerned with the long waiting list and the perception of poor quality care. Edgewater Health got the referral only as the place of last resort.

As luck would have it, I was hired by a *mostly* cooperative and understanding board of directors. And I say "mostly" cooperative with a heavy heart. There were a few board members who specialized in sabotage: undermining my decisions; putting restrictions on who could attend board meetings outside of the board; even playing the favored relative employee card. Most of them understood the role of the board as a governing body, and that of the CEO as the person to make the improvements happen. Having a good board was crucial to my ability to make desperately needed changes … and to make them quickly, before the doors were closed. My position was, "You hired me, so trust me, support me, and together we can turn this organization around."

To turn Edgewater Health around, I would have to make many changes.

There were disgruntled employees in cahoots with the bad board members; and some actively spawned rumors about my skills and personal life. They even lied about my previous employment. And, of course, there were always comments about "how I got the job" by sleeping with so and so. Some were even outraged that they weren't named the CEO. All garbage … but quite common for women in leadership positions to face.

The good news was that I had some excellent employees remain, many of whom had been there for a long time. They became a good source of historical knowledge about Edgewater. They shared what made Edgewater tick when it was working. Fortunately for me, these employees were committed to their jobs and the organization. These men and women had waited a long time for the missing ingredient to show up: leadership.

Gary, Indiana, was hit harder than most sections of the Midwest with the economic woes of the mid '90s. People in the area were in serious need of the services that a well-run community mental health center could offer. There was an available market of clients right outside our doors if they knew about us, and felt we could provide excellent services.

The center was housed in a lovely facility—a beautiful and substantial structure built in the early 1980s that had a good foundation. Although the physical plant was sound, overall maintenance needed upgrading immediately. The furniture was old, slightly shabby, and in need of cleaning. In truth, it all needed to be replaced.

Now it was up to me and the team that I would assemble to make good on what the community expected of us.

I didn't go into the situation blindly. I knew from the outset that I did not have the full support of the leadership team. Further, I knew many felt strongly that one of their own should have become the CEO. I received a lot of advance advice. Notes and telephone calls were sent to me by staff and others:

Get rid of this one ….

Move that one out ….

Keep this person ....

Fire that person ....

I made it a priority not to bring any negative or biased attitudes in with me when I walked through the door my first day on the job. My position was:

> We start from here and we start fresh. Everyone has a chance to shine. We are all here to turn this organization around and make it responsive, successful, and profitable. The goal was to become an invaluable resource in the community. One that others would refer to without hesitation.

Team members were challenged. "Show me what you can do, and we'll start from there," became my motto.

Often CEOs will take on a new position and immediately begin installing their own people as the management team right away. I had no desire to do so. The historical knowledge that many of them possessed could prove to be invaluable. And it was.

Because of the generally poor reputation of the organization, it was difficult to find quality replacements.

I did bring in a consultant with expertise in the field to provide support, assistance, and to serve as a sounding board in the first few months on the job. After all, I knew this would be a daunting task. The organization had a probationary state certification and was not nationally accredited, which was required by industry regulation. It had to be dealt with immediately.

The first step was to create several policies and procedures to guide us. Those who could not adjust to the changes began to move on. *I did not have to fire anyone.* As people came to accept the new way of doing things, most got on board. Others left of their own volition, unable to adapt to the new ways of doing business.

Their departures, as welcomed as they were, posed an unexpected problem. Because of the generally poor reputation of the organization, it was difficult to find quality replacements. I had to convince a lot of people that things had changed at Edgewater. It was initially a hard sell. Time helped. I began to enjoy more and more success, and recruitment became easier. I had to constantly reassure potential recruits that things were much better and together we could make the organization a place with a highly regarded reputation. And they would be part of making that happen.

Little by little, I began to build a team of loyal employees who shared the same values and goal of making the center a success. Those who were talented were promoted. Employees at all levels participated in sharing their ideas and opinions. "This is not my show," I told them. "This is OUR show. It's not up to me alone. It's up to all of us to make this work."

It was vindication for all of our efforts.

My approach worked, and we began to make great strides as a team. Staff began to get excited and motivated. I was honest with them. I let them know that with hard work and commitment, we would be certified and accredited within two years. But I also told them that if we failed, it was likely that the doors would close and their jobs would be gone.

The first realization that we had turned the corner came eighteen months later. It was vindication for all our efforts. Edgewater was awarded a three-year accreditation by a national accrediting body. Just one month later, we received state certification. These were heady moments for all of us, rewards for a lot of very hard work by a lot of dedicated people.

There was no time to rest on our laurels. We were far from finished. We needed the community and others in the industry to view us differently. After all, we needed business (clients) to stay afloat. Our goal: we wanted to be perceived among the best in providing healthcare services in the immediate geographic area. It was the least our customers and the community could expect from us, and the least that could be expected from ourselves.

Initially, efforts were focused on improving internal operations. Now it was time to take our message to the streets. We wanted everyone to know we were still here and ready to get to work addressing the healthcare needs of people in the community. Our senior leadership team began meeting with key stakeholders to tell the Edgewater story by:

- Letting the community know that we fully understood past problems and had worked hard to overcome them.

- Acknowledging that we were far from perfect but striving every day to be better than the day before.

- Being honest.

- Admitting that we might stumble a few times, but we were committed to getting it right.

The community heard us.

From the beginning, it was not easy to overcome public opinion. It was something that I attempted to keep an eye on. The next step was to gain the community's trust. Surprisingly, we discovered that many simply didn't know we existed. And unfortunately, others felt we were the last place they would turn to for help or a job because of previously poor leadership and mismanagement.

Once we received our accreditation and certification, it became easier because we had accomplished something we deliberately set out to do. It was obvious to most people that we were on the move once again and that we weren't all lip service. Edgewater Health had made a significant turnaround. The community took notice and celebrated with us.

Today, Edgewater Health is a $20 million organization and growing. We added additional services and now have expanded to ten locations in several communities. We extended our healthcare options to include primary care, e.g., family medicine, and pediatrics.

We are proud to say, "We treat the whole person." These changes and the subsequent growth have not been without additional challenges. But we've learned that with teamwork and commitment to success, nothing can keep us down.

Can I have done it alone? No.

—Dr. Danita Johnson Woods

the **Leader's Checklist**

Turnarounds and successes never happen overnight, nor can one person do it alone. Without the right people with the right attitudes and skill sets, our turnaround would not have happened.

Is It Your IQ, EQ, or PQ?

Leaders Educate, Empower, and Elevate

Leaders know the difference between important and urgent.

Many would-be leaders miss this deeper principle: *To be a leader you must have influence over your followers.*

It's easy to get someone to follow you. That's because roles and hierarchies within organizations make leadership transactional. "Joe, this is your new boss, Anita. Follow her." Does that always work … the follow someone approach? Or is there more?

There's more. It's up to you to make leadership more than just transactional. First and foremost, it must be relational. Your relationship with your followers is the optimum place where true leadership occurs and thrives.

This is especially true when leading through change. And when is a leader not managing some type of change?

Leading through change is not easy. I've held leadership positions for more than three decades. Those years continually remind me that leading through change is not easy. It's chaotic at times; it's overwhelming at other times.

Employees can practice the art of resistance. Change is rarely easy. Some changes are welcomed, while others are met with skepticism. While leading Edgewater through change, the biggest dilemma I faced was how to get people to accept the discomfort of change and follow me into an unknown future?

There were four essential elements to successfully implement and integrate the change process and the final change.

1. *Leaders realize that people must be prioritized.* At the most basic level of human interaction, people want to be seen, heard, and understood. Many leaders overlook this and leap straight into action plans and goals. Slow down. Spend time getting to know your people. Think about who they are, where they fit in the organization, what they dream and hope for, what they fear, and what contributions they want to make.

> **I needed to create a sense of urgency among the team.**

2. *Leaders know the difference between important and urgent.* Urgent usually demands immediate attention and has a time line. Important, on the other hand, may not have an impending deadline, but it does impact the organization's long-term strategic goals.

Most don't enjoy the disruption of change. Employees don't head to work thinking: *Today will be a fantastic day of chaos, confusion, and uncertainty. It will be fun and relaxing.* And, neither do you as a leader.

But, you have a goal. It is to shift them from wanting things to be better to being *willing* to make things better. You do this by helping them to understand what is important and what is urgent. When I became the CEO of Edgewater Health, I needed to create a sense of urgency among the team and clearly articulate why the threats to the organization's survival made immediate change necessary. That message needed to be communicated with clarity and confidence. Spelling out the direct consequences of ignoring needed change for so long had now made the situation urgent.

Nothing has helped me more in my career than understanding the difference between those things that are important compared to those things that are urgent. Important problems or tasks are the things that contribute to an organization's mission and goals. These are the things that we do every day to sustain and validate our presence. Those things that are urgent though, command immediate attention.

3. *Embrace a spirit of possibility.* Leaders who look to the future with an open mind, innovation, and renewed thinking can inspire their teams to envision and work toward what could be. They have the potential to create organizations that are not only successful, but organizations that thrive. Team members become excited about sharing their ideas and about shaping the organization's future.

Leaders who embody a spirit of possibility are optimistic and open to the many unknown opportunities that have not yet been revealed. They have faith in and inspire their team. And because they do, they get better results. If you view your workspace as full of challenges, defects, and barriers, it will stifle the excitement of the team and stir reluctance in the team's desire to put forth its best efforts.

Embracing a spirit of possibility is empowering to an organization and the teams within it. When your employees are excited about the direction of the organization, they are motivated to give their best. When they are excited, they feel that their contributions are valued. The result: Going to work each day is enjoyable and exciting to them because they know they are making a difference. The benefits to such an approach are immeasurable.

4. *Leaders make decisions even when the decisions are unpopular.* I've had varying degrees of success in my leadership career. Sometimes, things have not always gone perfectly. Even after my decades of experience, I continue to learn and grow as a leader. And in the ever-changing industry of health care, Edgewater Health must be flexible and nimble to maneuver all that comes its way.

Sometimes leadership requires making hard decisions and choosing a path that goes against the norm. It takes courage. It has been said that the lack of courage, in management and in life, is perhaps the most critical factor in determining whether you will succeed or fail as a leader. Organizations today need leaders who are unencumbered by fear. More courageous leaders are needed who can guide them through troubled times, despite the challenges, and help organizations serve up successful turnarounds. And leaders are needed who can make hard decisions.

Change in business is inevitable.

Sometimes you'll win and sometimes you'll chalk up a bad decision as a learning opportunity. As a leader you will always have to make decisions. In business, be unapologetic about the decisions you make even if they don't work out as planned. Thinking through your decisions carefully and always using your best judgment, based on the information you've been able to gather, is unquestionably the best that you can do. Doing your research and using your best reasoning will take you and those who work with and for you far … opening doors to places in your career path that you hadn't imagined.

Unplanned vs Planned Change

Change is about personal growth. As a leader, you are better equipped to master change in the workplace if you can master change in your personal life. On a different level, these days it seems that the words "business" and "change" go hand in hand. Your motto should be that change in business is inevitable.

For our leadership team, it was exhausting.

There was no better example of the planned vs the unplanned than what happened when COVID-19 reared its head. Traditional workplaces were turned upside down and inside out. The sanctuary of the home was no longer a sanctuary. It was transformed into "the boss's business workplace" plus sleeping quarters plus childcare facility for those who used to take their kids to child care while they went to "work" to homeschooling to you name it. "Zoom" and "zooming" became the most used words for anyone who worked. Zoom fatigue became a new malady.

A pandemic wasn't on my radar … and I bet it wasn't on yours. I scrambled to make sure that my remote employees had the wi-fi they needed; the necessary bandwidth for it; extra phone lines and phones; the ability to access our internal networks by getting security protected computers; and new training. And the training extended to our patients. We had to train them on how to use the technology that for some was like learning a foreign language. It was exhausting for our leadership team.

There are basically two types of change that leaders are confronted with almost daily. When organizations make intentional decisions about the operations, these are considered planned changes. These can be things such as planning the organization's business strategy or goals. On the other hand, unplanned change is a result of unanticipated occurrences, from dealing with a key executive quitting or a public relations disaster, to new customer demands and regulatory changes. Sudden and externally mandated changes affect organizations of all sizes.

Both planned and unplanned change can be externally or internally driven. As you cope with change in your environment, it can cause stress. When change is forced upon you, making the shift is often more stressful and more difficult than when you thoughtfully decide to take your organization in a new direction. After all, making a change that you plan for is exciting and filled with opportunity, while the unplanned change can put you on a roller coaster experience.

Unplanned change can put you on a roller coaster experience.

Opportunity and excitement can lead to stress as well. But typically, this kind of stress is good because it motivates you. It can focus your energy and improve your performance. Because it is planned, you have control over the pace of the change and so it feels manageable.

Making a change because of external pressure is often filled with risk and unpredictability. This type of stress is perceived as outside of your control. It can create an overwhelmed sense and decrease your motivation. This type of stress usually feels unpleasant.

Unfortunately, most organizations are slow to respond, resisting these external pressures to change. They fear the risk involved, and as a result they miss opportunities. Change under external circumstances is scary because your buy-in to the new ideas is often tentative, and as such, you don't know if the changes you're making are going to work. Additionally, the change may mean you have to alter your organization's values or culture, and those sorts of changes don't come easy.

The Organization Change Process

Embracing any type of change, either planned or unplanned, requires both courage and flexibility.

The following are tips for making the organizational change process easier, less stressful, and more successful.

TIP 1: *Curiosity informs your leadership perspective.*
Create an environment that encourages continuous learning. Encourage your team members to learn about what is going on in their industry and to stay abreast of changes in their field.

Myrtle Campbell is a good friend. She doesn't work in health care. Instead, she brings a perspective as a retired public school superintendent. She shared,

> I wish I had known the long-term impact that the proliferation of Charter Schools would have on public schools, particularly in Gary, Indiana. The influx of charter schools prompted a change in state and federal regulations, school financing, the school funding formula and diverted needed funds from public education. In addition, licensing standards for teachers and administrators were lowered to accommodate the staffing at charters.

As someone who was as deeply involved with educating children as Myrtle was, the changes to allow charter schools to infiltrate the public school space was a cause of much consternation in the education arena. I know … it was a common topic in our break rooms at Edgewater. Parents and grandparents buzzed about it.

As a leader, it's sometimes not possible to know these things ahead of time. But, sometimes keeping your ears and eyes open can give you a heads up for planning purposes and gives you an opportunity to adjust mentally.

Wise leaders encourage their teams to have the courage to ask the dumb questions. Do you? After all, if an individual team member is confused, chances are there may be others on the team who are as well. Always seek clarification. Clarity in communication and goals is essential to a team's effectiveness.

Know that it's okay to change your mind. New experiences, new information, changes in circumstances can change your perspective. Having as much information as you can get will help to inform your decision making. This will give you the confidence needed to forge ahead.

And remember, you don't have to have all the answers. It's okay to reach out for support and to spend time doing more research. We all have access to close friends, counselors, and advisors who can add value to our understanding. These confidants, mentors, or coaches are invaluable to a leader's mental health and confidence.

The knowledge you and your team possess has long-term value for the organization. If you stop learning, you stop having the ability to contribute to the continued development of the organization. Learning is vital because things change so quickly —technology changes, the industry changes, the marketplace changes. You should keep up and know what's state-of-the-art to stay relevant to your customers. The more learning opportunities people have, the more valued they'll feel, and the more they'll want to contribute to the change process.

TIP 2: *Hold people to their commitments.*
No matter how good the planning is, change will never be complete if responsibilities are abandoned midstream. That's why you need to hold your people accountable for what they commit to—as well as yourself. To do so, first make sure they have the skills needed to do the job and any equipment they need. If they don't, there's no way they'll be successful. If I hadn't done what I did with new phones, computers, equipment, trainings for our team during the pandemic, our company would not have survived.

Next, get employees to feel some sense of ownership to the task before them. If possible, let them volunteer for tasks rather than assign them. If that's not possible, then let them create their own plan to complete the tasks, or at the very least, get their input on how the job needs to be done. The more they feel they have control over the job to be done, the more likely they are to complete it.

Monitor their progress and evaluate how they are contributing—or not contributing—to the change process. Your monitoring doesn't mean micromanaging. And it does not mean that you are a *snoopervisor*, as opposed to a supervisor. It simply means you are continually taking the pulse of the entire workflow to ensure that all of the pieces of the process fit together and are being accomplished. When you find that someone isn't contributing effectively, it usually means the big picture isn't understood and how his or her work plays into the overall goal or change. If someone is lacking, you must be willing to confront the situation, dealing with it in a constructive way that gets the work back on track. If you don't, it affects your entire team.

TIP 3: *Be clear, consistent, and continuous when communicating the vision and goals and the why of the change.*
In messaging, the savvy leader is clear and consistent about the change: about what's occurring; about what needs to occur; and about the vision and goals for the company. *Is that you?* Start with saying where the company is going as well as the plan to get there as specifically as possible and in language that is clear and consistent. Connect each person's role or task

back to the overall goal so he or she can fully understand and embrace the outcome of the forthcoming change. Encourage them to ask questions and, if possible, to contribute to the message. Not surprisingly, solutions can come from within and by those who are impacted. Again, others will buy into an idea more easily if they feel they took part in shaping it.

When you are not clear and consistent, your message gets distorted, and people don't understand it. That's when problems happen, and change becomes risky. You think you're communicating one thing, but no one understands your real message. The outcome is that resistance builds and they may be pulled in a different direction. It is important that employees are on the same page as it relates to their need to understand the direction of the organization and the why behind it.

Be prepared to communicate multiple times. Don't just transmit your message once. Instead, continuously revisit it and make sure everyone is still clear on why the change is in force. And since everyone learns and processes information differently, it may mean you have to communicate the message in various mediums.

Various mediums might include: verbally talking about the change; writing it out in report form; creating a multimedia video that shows the change; holding a type of company or team town hall; or communicating it in any other way that engages the different learning styles of auditory, visual, and kinesthetic personalities. The goal is to get everyone moving in the same direction. This makes holding them accountable much easier.

Approach Change Proactively

Change that is mandated from outside factors is often uncomfortable, but this doesn't mean it's a bad thing. In fact, when approached correctly, an outside factor change can open your eyes to new possibilities, new customer bases, new revenue streams, and even new product and service offerings.

And here's a plus: When you challenge and deal with these externally influenced changes proactively, you'll have the upper hand. Not only will you fare better than your competitors during the change, but you could emerge as an industry leader. And that's one change you want to occur.

As a leader, be open to change.
Without it, you will stagnate.

—Dr. Danita Johnson Woods

the **Leader's Checklist**

Your goal is to shift people from wanting things to be better to being willing to make things better.

Influence ... Your Superpower

To be a leader you must have influence over your followers.

Every leader is tasked with the work of bringing along her followers through influence and persuasion … every one of them. To have impact, she must inspire, teach, and encourage her employees, consumers, and stakeholders to follow her, often into unfamiliar or even scary places.

Leaders influence others in several ways … from group meetings or presentations, one-on-one sessions with individuals, acting as a mentor, written communications, published work, even within interviews conducted by the media. Always, the goal is to connect with the listeners or viewers in ways that will inspire and engage them to act in a way that will benefit the greater good.

Inspiring and impactful leadership is not about unilateral decision making and strategy. You could do that all by yourself, by acting autonomously, and by counting on the efforts of others. But would others follow through as you'd expect? Would they convey your vision and strategy as you wanted it? In most cases, a leader of influence wants to convince others to come along with her on a journey that may require some risk taking or going against the grain. This is frequently the case when leading through change and navigating new or even hostile environments.

Your relationship with your followers is the optimum place where true leadership occurs.

To be a leader, you must have influence over your followers.

Getting someone to follow you can be easy. Organization structure, roles, and hierarchies are there to make the job easy. But sometimes leadership can be challenging. Having successful relationships with those you lead can help you to overcome these challenges. That's because organization success is built on relationships within the workplace. True leadership thrives in an organization where relationships are valued and cultivated. Inspiring leaders are shaped by a true compassion for a cause, or when staring in the face of adversity. One such leader is arguably the first black millionaire. Madam C.J. Walker was the first black female millionaire in America and enjoyed her affluence and influence thanks to her own line of homemade haircare products targeted specifically to black women.

She was born as Sarah Breedlove on the same plantation where her parents were sharecroppers in Delta, Louisiana, on December 23, 1867. Of her four siblings, she was the first to be born free from slavery after the Emancipation Proclamation was passed. By the age of seven, she was orphaned. By fourteen, she was married, allegedly due to early hardships and to have a place of her own. By the time she was twenty, her husband had passed away leaving her to care for her two-year-old daughter on her own.

After her husband's death, Sarah moved to St. Louis to live with her three brothers who were all barbers. For more than a decade, she worked as a poorly paid washerwoman while attending night school. A brief time later, she experienced a scalp disorder and started to lose her hair. She also noticed that lots of other black women had the same hair problem as she did.

Sarah traded her washerwoman status for a sales agent job working with Annie Malone, a black hair entrepreneur. During her sales agent experience, two things happened. Sarah recognized that she had a gift for selling, and she met Charles J. Walker, her husband-to-be.

Her observations revealed several things that black women had in common: poor hygiene; food consumption was limited to scraps and mediocre quality; and scalp diseases were prevalent. For the black woman, if there was dandruff, it meant that the hair was brittle and falling out.

The black neighborhoods of St. Louis were her stomping grounds

It was time for her to break out on her own.

as she started selling products directly to black women door-to-door, teaching women how to groom and style their hair.

She then moved to Denver, still selling Annie Malone's hair products, and finally married Charles James Walker.

Because of her own hair loss, she began experimenting with many ingredients and finally came up with a secret formula to stimulate hair growth and take care of the dandruff as well. A more frequent cleansing of the hair and scalp combined with her "secret formula" that included sulfur, produced remarkable results for her and other women who volunteered to use her treatments.

Recognizing remarkable results achieved by those using her products, Sarah knew that she had created "a cure" for women just like her. It was time for her to break out on her own and create her own haircare products.

Sarah was a shameless self-promoter.

Eventually, her products would change the face of the black haircare industry. Her methods were known as the "Walker System," of hair care.

She learned quickly that she was a gifted entrepreneur with a flair for self-promotion. Sarah was a shameless self-promoter. Because of her product's increasing recognition as a "miracle cure," in time, she was able to influence several thousand agents around the country to sell her full line of products for growing and beautifying hair. Madam C.J. Walker's products sold for 50 cents … today that would be equivalent to $15!

Her husband, Charles "C.J." Walker was skilled in marketing and promotion. He suggested that she needed a name of substance: Madam C.J. Walker … and Madam C.J. Walker she became. He helped her to understand and use the power of advertising and brand awareness to her advantage. Her face was shown prominently on her product containers. She advertised heavily in black newspapers and magazines. She traveled extensively to promote her products and recruit women for her sales force.

The self-made millionaire used her wealth to fund scholarships for women at the Tuskegee Institute and donated large parts of her wealth to the NAACP, the black YMCA, and other charities.

She relocated to Indianapolis, Indiana, where she believed her business could flourish. As an advocate of black women's economic independence, she opened training programs teaching the "Walker System" to her national network of licensed sales agents who earned healthy commissions. Her company claimed to have trained nearly 20,000 women.

Her influence with her agents expanded beyond sales in the black community. In addition to training in sales and grooming, Walker showed other black women how to budget, build their own businesses, and encouraged them to become financially independent.

Madame C.J. Walker convened her first conference during a Philadelphia summer. There were 200 women in attendance. It is believed to have been among the first national gatherings of women entrepreneurs to discuss business and commerce.

She was also very charitable and gave back to her community by contributing to black organizations in Indianapolis. She encouraged others to do so as well and rewarded those who made the largest contributions to charities to encourage their continued generosity to communities and organizations where they lived and worked. At the convention, women who had the highest sales volume and brought in the greatest number of new sales agents received prizes.

Most of her activities were aimed toward education and building of personal and racial pride. She also became actively involved in fighting against prejudice and discrimination. Through her influence, she encouraged her agents to develop their own political strength and become political and social activists to promote civil and human rights.

Through her innovation, hard work, entrepreneurship, benevolence, and concern for the well-being of others, Madam Walker was able to influence and change the lives of thousands of women. She died on May 25, 1919.

Leadership is about being an influencer of things big and small.

Her legacy still is celebrated today by persons seeking to make their own mark in the business world. Her personal influence was her superpower. It has impacted many and spanned several generations.

The Persuasion Factor

Have you ever been wrapped up in what you thought was a great idea? Or think you have a brilliant way to solve a difficult problem by the sheer force of your will?

Did it work? Or did it bomb?

My personal definition of leadership is using the power of persuasion to ethically influence others to change their behavior to get things done. It's not uncommon for would-be leaders to forget their most important task is to positively impact the lives of others so that they will want to accomplish more.

A true leader provides a solution or solves a problem presented. It may require that you engage others in your efforts. And often, it's more than just delegating to someone else to fix the problem.

First, it's always about them ... your team members. You may think it's about you ... but it's not—at least in their eyes and those are the eyes to come through for continual growth of your team ... or your organization. Leadership lessons from world-class leaders clearly illustrate the need to frame your desires in ways that will inspire others to want to change their behaviors. A leader must instill a personal, internal desire to work toward a goal and to achieve success as a matter of personal conviction. To do so, you must remember that little things do count. Little things go a long way, such as referring to your employees by name and showing that you value their contributions to the team and the organization.

Employees remember compliments that come from their leaders.

Employees remember compliments that come from their leaders. Never undervalue the power of recognition. A bonus to you: Those little things that seem trivial will increase your popularity among the ranks. And, with increased acceptance and esteem comes more influence. Influence is essential when change is being integrated.

Leadership is about being an influencer of things big and small. In fact, being able to influence others is one of the most powerful and challenging tools of a leader. It's about spurring people into action through positive persuasion and encouragement. Being influential makes for an exceptional, rather than a good, leader. As an exceptional leader, you inspire and energize your team to want more, do more, and be more.

By positively influencing others, you empower them to freely contribute to the success of the organization. By demonstrating respect for their ideas and opinions they feel valued. After all, if you want to get things done, and no one is following you, you aren't influencing them at all. Don't underestimate the influence factor. It is an important and necessary quality that is required to be a great leader.

Leadership is about knowing that without followers, there are no leaders.

Without influence, leaders have little to no followers. Your followers are the generators of ideas and solutions. Leaders know that within that collective effort lies accomplishment. To achieve victories—big and small—you must interact positively with individual members of your team. Building on these individual relationships will raise your level of influence with the group.

Remember, you can have the most fantastic, innovative ideas in the world, but if you cannot succeed in getting the buy-in of those you are attempting to lead, then all your efforts will ultimately fall short. It's about the people you are attempting to lead—always.

- What do they see you do to support them?
- What do they hear you say that has substance and action behind your words?
- What do they hear you say or see you do that undermines those actions and/or words?

By definition, a leader has people behind her. If she does not, she is not a leader. A leader spends enormous amounts of time considering the landscapes of the minds and hearts of the people she is trying to lead. The secret of being a successful leader relies on your ability to get people to follow you on a challenging journey to a new, unknown place that is far outside of their usual comfort zones. And they follow without resistance. Oh, there can be questions. That's for clarity. Communicate with confidence and move them forward.

Purposeful and meaningful change often requires a collective effort.

Do you know who you are trying to lead? Is it everyone in the organization … or a specific group? As a leader there are a variety of things you need to take into consideration about those you wish to lead. A great leader always assesses the individuals on the team that she has been given the privilege to lead.

Questions to start with include:

- Who are the members of your team?

- What are their strengths and shortcomings?

- Are they new to leadership or are they seasoned leaders?

- What do they like to do for fun?

- Are they frequently stressed or most often engaged and happy?

- What fears do they have?

- What are their dreams and what do they want to accomplish personally and professionally?

- How will they feel about a new way of doing things?

- Are they excited about a novel approach or are they afraid or even adverse to the idea of change?
- What pushbacks are you likely to encounter?
- Do they see you as a leader who is able to take, as well as receive constructive feedback?
- What concerns, questions or insecurities do they have?
- How will they feel about you?
- What is your track record as a leader?
- Will you always bring the best version of yourself?
- Are you trustworthy?
- Are you known or unknown to them?
- Are you considered a good listener?
- Are you seen as thoughtful?
- Will they see you as a know-it-all or will they see you as an innovator?
- Will they believe that you are keeping their best interests at heart, or will they tag you as self-interested?

Spend time getting to know the people you want to lead before you try to lead them. Knowing these things can help you build an effective team and achieve incredible results.

When you truly consider the human side of those you lead, you are well on your way to being a phenomenal leader.

—Dr. Danita Johnson Woods

the **Leader's Checklist**

As an influencer, you empower your team members to drive much needed change for the organization to be successful. Purposeful and meaningful change often requires a collective effort. Whether it's a goal, solving a problem or completing a task, connecting with people is the key to organizational success.

Effectively engaging employees involves providing the tools they need to succeed. Whether they need support, or additional resources, you must find out what they need and seek to ensure that they have it in abundance to help them stay motivated to put forth their best effort and achieve the goals you have set.

Delusion is a deadly trait in a leader.

A strong leader builds trust and rapport with her employees by helping them feel more confident in working as a team to solve problems. Having unclouded vision about where you're going as an organization, and providing clear direction and support encourages team members to complete projects and tasks on time. The work is also made much less burdensome when team members know that they have a strong leader directing, guiding, and monitoring their efforts and one who is there to support them, or catch and redirect them should they fall short.

You should spend time seriously considering each of the above concepts: listening, goal setting, and influence. It is imperative that you be brutally honest with yourself. Delusion is a deadly trait in a leader. If you are a bad listener, admit it and start being a good one. If you are unknown to these folks, don't assume they will love you because of your beautiful smile or your gregarious personality.

Ask yourself how you would feel if you were leading you! When it is a question of how others see you, remember that for better or worse, perception is often reality.

Emotional Grit ... a Leader's Secret Sauce

Most everyone is called to lead at some point in his/her life.

So many people don't think of themselves as leaders because they lack formal training and/or recognized education degrees. Take Bridget Cheatham, a billing supervisor with a dozen individuals who report to her and take guidance. She has no formal degree. Her skills were learned on the job and from the school of hard knocks.

Bridget is organized; follows through with all her assignments; and doesn't drop surprises on her team members. Whether she is interacting one-on-one within her total team, she actively encourages questions. She isn't a "tell you" leader ... she's a "show you" leader so that her team members can "get" what she's demonstrating. One thing that Bridget advocates for is ongoing interactive training. She doesn't want anyone left behind.

Bridget didn't plan on any job that would lead to her being called a leader, at least consciously. Yet, most everyone is called to lead at some point in his/her life.

And Bridget went through the door when it was opened to her. For you, it may have been in fourth grade when you were called upon by your teacher to be a hall monitor. Or, it could have been when your high school peers encouraged you to run for class president.

Regardless of how you enter the leadership realm, you are being called to serve. Service, more than anything else, is what makes a good leader successful. Those passionate, enthusiastic, and committed individuals who see leadership as their purpose are destined to become the great leaders. It's like a calling.

It can be like herding cats and mice.

Leading organizations today offers significant challenges for leaders at any experience level as they attempt to lead through uncertain and even turbulent times. As leaders attempt to effectuate change, especially in organizations that are satisfied with the status quo, it demands a great deal from them. And it demands grit—*Emotional Grit.*

Most quickly learn that a specific set of required skills are needed to be successful in the job. If the leadership track is where you want to be, an assessment is needed to determine what skills you currently have; what skills you lack; and what skills you need to acquire.

Being a great leader requires a tremendous amount of Emotional Grit.

Whether you have these skills intuitively or learn them by delving head-on into the job, you must be able to inspire and motivate people to be effective. It's not easy. It never is. It can be like herding cats and mice. No matter how difficult the task, your job is to identify the vision, establish the goals, then direct and lead your team into the organization of the future.

But not everyone has the stomach to be a leader.

- Leadership can be hard.

- It can be demanding.

- It can be frustrating.

But it can also be rewarding and even enjoyable if you have the right attitude, skill set, and commitment. Being a great leader requires a tremendous amount of *Emotional Grit. Emotional Grit* is the unshakeable determination and commitment to persist and move toward your goals, your passion, even in the face of obstacles.

If you think about it, being a leader can be tough. It requires the development of many personal characteristics that do not automatically or suddenly appear in a person's life. It requires maturation, tenacity, and a willingness to fail on occasion, and then regroup and get right back at it.

To keep at it even when the challenges seem overwhelming, a leader needs to develop a powerful sense of *Emotional Grit.*

Emotional Grit is a firmness of purpose or steadfastness. It's knowing who you are; what your vision is for your team and for the organization; and having the tenacity to follow through and stick it out, even when it gets ugly.

Emotional Grit means having a firm decision or goal and an unwavering pursuit for achieving it. A student might have a goal to be the first in her family to get a college degree, no matter how long it takes her or how hard she must work. Her determination gives her the motivation to wake up early to study, push through fatigue and boredom while completing her class assignments and to keep moving forward when she wants to quit. Her grit and determination spur her on through dozens of other factors that threaten her resolve.

Emotional Grit gives you hope. Throughout your life, you may be tempted at times to quit. You may want to drop a class when the assignment is hard or give up your diet when you're struggling to eat healthy. Giving up is easy, but fortunately, you have a tool on your side that can help—Emotional Grit. Emotional Grit is incredibly powerful during challenging times.

Emotional Grit spurs creativity. If you come across a roadblock or run out of options, you can become frustrated. However, determination spurs creativity and encourages you to produce creative solutions to complex problems.

Emotional Grit pushes you to go above and beyond. When you want something bad enough, you are willing to go the extra mile to achieve it. This is Emotional Grit in action! A person with Emotional Grit knows the time and effort put into doing something that is challenging is worthwhile if the goal is reached.

> **A woman of Emotional Grit does not throw herself a pity party and invite other commiserate souls to attend.**

Emotional Grit helps you motivate others. A leader with Emotional Grit is an optimist. She often rallies other people, convincing them that even though the work is hard and there is a lot to do, it can be done, if everyone works together. It's the determination of the optimist that motivates people to work harder until the end.

Emotional Grit provides guidance and inspiration. A leader with Emotional Grit is actively engaged and wants the best for herself, her team, and her organization. Instead of disconnecting and choosing to be uninvolved, a leader with Emotional Grit encourages people to stay focused and driven to put forth their best efforts.

Are there specific traits of a woman with Emotional Grit? The answer is yes. I've identified ten Emotional Grit factors.

Emotional Grit for Women Leaders

1. She sets small goals for herself.

You cannot accomplish your goals all at once. No one completes a marathon without training. I know because I've done it— six times.

I started by running one mile, and then I kept building up my strength and my stamina until I reached a point where I could go the full 26.2 miles. When I finished that first marathon, I felt like I had been run over by a truck. But I was determined. So determined that I went on to do it five more times.

If you want to practice Emotional Grit, start by setting achievable goals for yourself.

2. She controls the things she can.

She knows that if she takes command of her own life, she sets herself up for success and limits the impact of forces she can't control. You can't control other people, but you can control your response. Don't focus on what may be perceived as the dark impulses of humanity. Instead, focus on your own self-control.

3. She doesn't whine or complain.

She doesn't let negativity pull her down. She does not complain about her circumstances or consider herself a victim. She pushes through no matter what, by focusing on the positive.

A woman of Emotional Grit does not throw herself a pity party and invite other commiserate souls to attend. Let go of regret. What's done is done. And don't let others cause you to keep revisiting past wrongs and hurt. Acknowledge your transgressions, make amends, and MOVE ON.

4. She is self-aware.

A woman of strong Emotional Grit has the courage to engage in an in-depth, personal analysis of any unpleasant circumstance she finds herself in and says, "Maybe it's me!"

Are you looking at your own actions and behavior first? If you are, you might ask yourself, *What is it that I could do differently or better?* You might also ask, *Even though it may not be my problem, what have I done to cause the problem to continue without any change?*

By asking yourself these questions, you begin to awaken to your own errors more quickly. It will help you to be better—personally and professionally.

This week, stop to consider the alternative to staying on the path you are now traveling. It could be disastrous unless you are willing to make a change. I am confident your eyes will be opened, and you will get in the right lane!

5. She manages her expectations to avoid disappointment.

She knows that she can't predict the future, but she can direct the trajectory of her life by being mindful of the choices she makes. Managing your expectations can give you a sense of peace and control. Things you can do to manage your expectations include:

- Set realistic goals.
- Accept others as they are and find a way to connect with them.
- Be flexible. Things don't always happen as you wish. Learn to adapt.
- Don't be too quick to judge others or their motivation. First, try to understand.
- Prepare for problems by expecting the unexpected.
- Avoid drama. If it doesn't improve your life, walk away.

6. She stands her ground.

She is not concerned with what other people think about her. She refuses to be bullied and stands up for herself. She is determined not to let her feathers get ruffled.

A woman woven with Emotional Grit focuses on reaching her personal goals. Only you can decide when to keep trying and when to step back. It's all up to you. Those that follow you know that you don't fail simply because you may occasionally lose a battle.

You only fail if you quit before you have explored all of your options. Failure equals opportunity. "Sometimes you win, sometimes you learn" becomes a mantra. You do not allow fear of failure to interfere with your plans.

7. She knows that most people have good intentions.

Have you ever gotten hung up on what you perceive as the manipulation and underhanded actions of others? If it occurs, you tend to take these things personally as if they are meant to bring about your personal demise. For example, you may be competing for a promotion along with one of your colleagues. Your colleague may remind Human Resources that you don't have the prerequisite years of experience. Your reaction might be to confront your colleague because you believe she has undermined you.

A valid "but" is inserted here. It may not be about you. Most people's actions are usually about them, e.g., *How can I get ahead? Will this impress my boss? How do others see me? What do others think about me?*

Their actions are normally meant to gain an advantage or to curry favor. Don't get caught up in believing that you are the target of some imaginary conspiracy.

8. She knows how to distance herself from an issue.

What if you've just gotten over a problem, are in the middle of one, or a problem is coming your way? A dear friend often says to me, "The best way to deal with challenges is to make friends with the problems in your life." This is the nature of life. Accept it and learn to deal with it.

Ask yourself, *Are my problems close to my heart and pre-venting me from being rational? Should I put them out on the table so I can be more objective about things rather than holding them in and agonizing while trying to think of a solution?*

Knowing that problems are inevitable and that everyone experiences challenges in life will help you to get through your trials more easily.

9. She knows no leader is immune from failure and many welcome it.

A failed idea, project, or decision is inevitable in any organization. No one wants to feel like a loser. Most fear the humiliation that comes from the embarrassment and worry that their reputation will somehow suffer.

As a leader, you know that there can be numerous reasons for a project or process to fail. Some failures are due to understandable errors, while others may be due to carelessness. A close examination of the cause of the error will usually reveal a lot. When errors occur, it is your job to assess the cause of the failure and determine next steps to get everyone back on track.

If you are willing to look critically at what happened, you may find that even failures can provide valuable insights and information. It can also help you and your team to grow as you begin to understand and build upon the knowledge gained from the analysis. And it may even leapfrog you to your next success.

10. She knows the value of self-care.

Taking wellness seriously is important to her emotional and physical health. Self-care is understood to be a privilege and a responsibility.

A woman of Emotional Grit knows that self-care is not being selfish. She engages in activities and behaviors that nourish her. She knows that self-care is not an emergency burnout prevention plan, a New Year's resolution, or a quick fix. She does not engage in actions that deplete her. Nor does she allow tasks to be added to her to-do list that will overwhelm her. She knows when to say "No."

A great leader has a powerful sense of purpose and a whole lot of Emotional Grit.

—Dr. Danita Johnson Woods

the **Leader's Checklist**

Many don't start out wanting to be a leader. But when you are called upon and given the privilege to lead, you must continuously inspire your team to strive for success and accomplishment. You must keep them motivated to come to work every day and make a difference. This is what makes you successful and your organization thrive.

6 Why Multiplication Is Better than Addition

Your plan must focus on developing and multiplying leaders within the organization.

While sitting in a sandwich shop in Ocho Rios, Jamaica, I glanced up and saw a sign. It read, "Life is like a sandwich. You have to fill it with the best ingredients."

And just like making a great sandwich, you need the right people to have the best team—your ingredients.

Monica Oss has managed a successful consulting practice for years. I once asked her what she wished she had known earlier in her career.

> My response is easy ... doing it is where the leader's smarts comes in. Hiring the right people is tricky. Be quicker to hire new managers and move current managers—and their positions—around in your organization until you get the 'right fit' in a role.

Just like making a sandwich, you might try several different condiments, meats, or cheeses before you get the right combination, but eventually you do get it right. And, just like making a great sandwich, a successful leader must evaluate the strengths and weaknesses of each team member to ensure the most workplace success. Otherwise, everything either stales or becomes rancid.

Monica added,

Over half your time needs to be spent making your team successful.

In other words, you must have an intentional plan—not just adding new and moving around existing team members. Your plan must focus on developing and multiplying leaders within the organization. As a leader, you will have the most significant impact when you are intentional and deliberate in your focus on leadership development. When you recruit good talent, focus on their personal and professional development, and raise them up as leaders, it can lead to limitless potential for what you can accomplish in your organization.

Simply adding new employees to your organization is not what you want.

Organizations today are experiencing high employee turnover. Turnover can be costly. When it occurs, you may have trouble finding replacements and retaining them once you have managed to get them on board. Sometimes expensive temps are brought in, and productivity can decline.

Having a leadership development pipeline could be the answer to these types of challenges. I know that recruitment for key positions can be grueling. But even so, I often tell my team,

We don't want just another warm body. We want people who understand and value our mission and who are on board with our vision. We want people who desire to continue to grow.

Simply adding new people to your organization is not what you want. What you want are people who have the skills and discipline to internalize the mission and vision of your organization, align themselves with your values and help you create and sustain healthy growth.

If you add new, warm bodies to your team because they have a good resume, it doesn't always add to your organization's strategic and sustainable growth. In fact, it can limit your growth and expansion opportunities. It requires foresight and intentionality to develop leaders who are cohesive and capable of carrying out the mission and objectives.

Growing the numbers of your leadership team isn't the answer either. Instead, you want to create the potential for unlimited growth opportunities for your team through training and development. Multiplying capable leaders creates the potential for those leaders to multiply other leaders, resulting in your organization's success for many years. It starts with you—producing better leaders through focused effort, who in turn produce new leaders that ultimately go on reproducing leaders themselves. The result: A persistent and dynamic organizational process is woven throughout.

Some leaders feel that they need to be the smartest about every subject … about everything. In meetings, they frequently interrupt others to show off their prowess. They often suck all the creative energy from a room. Team members may quickly become disenchanted and feel undervalued. In turn, they shut down, feeling stifled and underappreciated. These "smartest" style leaders are found in almost every organization, perhaps even yours.

On the other hand, the best leaders are those who are secure enough in their own abilities and knowledge that they focus their efforts on growing and developing their team members. Their purpose is to expand their knowledge and skill sets to create a pool of talented leaders by fostering a culture of continual learning. This reservoir of talent can be invaluable in times of critical position turnover and can lessen the impact of loss of institutional knowledge. Obviously filling a vacated position from existing talent makes the transition much smoother.

If your organization is like mine, Edgewater Health, we have limited resources. For us to conduct our mission and vision, my leadership team must frequently garner the capabilities of existing employees to increase productivity and grow the organization. In fact, a frequent mantra among the team is *we are doing more with less*. Does that sound familiar?

Doing more with less is one way that we multiply our leaders—by encouraging them to stretch their abilities and learn new skills. Leadership author John C. Maxwell writes, "Multiplying leaders is the single greatest investment you can make because it produces the single greatest return."

By multiplying leaders, the burden of the workload will be shared.

Organizations today cannot afford to become dependent on one individual to guide the ship and drop the anchor at the same time. This can lead to burnout, decreased morale, disengagement, and premature turnover. Leaders must focus on the big picture while encouraging collaboration, independent decision making and empowering members of the team to move forward. By multiplying leaders, the burden of the workload will be shared, and you will continue to nurture and expand the talent in your leadership pool.

For your organization to move to its next level of greatness, you must grow your people. You don't have a choice … unless your goal is to go out of business.

Training them in critical decision-making skills and empowering them to act when called, allows them to creatively solve problems without the need of a senior level manager to always intervene. Such a strategy ensures that all employees are actively engaged and working toward a common purpose—sustainability and strategic organization growth.

> **Successful leaders are forged from the white-hot fires of life experience.**

Stepping into Leadership

There is no official playbook for being a good leader. There are countless programs that teach the theory of managing people. Many provide excellent training for persons seeking to begin a career in leadership and others provide advanced studies for those who want to learn more. But in my three plus decades as a leader, I've learned that successful leaders are forged from the white-hot fires of life experience. And experience comes from the trenches … not the tower looking down.

On occasion you might get singed, but you must treat the injury and keep moving. You keep pushing through the discomfort knowing that much of life is about trial and error. Mistakes and mishaps are part of the process in growing as a leader.

Transitioning from coworker to leader is common in organizations looking to promote the best and the brightest within the ranks. But it often represents new and uncomfortable challenges for those newly appointed and often unseasoned managers. The learning curve is often steep, especially when you are not given the right supports, and this is often the case when positions are filled through internal promotions.

As a first-time leader, you might be uncertain about how well you will work out in your new position. You may be filled with trepidation about your new role. And a feeling of insecurity is not uncommon. You may even begin to question your abilities. All are classic symptoms of imposter syndrome: You are faking it until you make it.

As a leader who is experiencing the imposter syndrome, you might be burdened with doubt and become consumed with negative thoughts like:

- *I am not supposed to be here …*

- *I am not worthy …*

- *I am not qualified …*

- *I'll never figure it out …*

- *I'm the only one who doesn't have it together …*

- *I don't have the right skills or talent …*

- *I am out of my lane …*

These are textbook examples of phrases that underlie the imposter syndrome, especially for women, and they are self-imposed. Anyone new to management can become a slave to the imposter syndrome. If you don't have the right tools that are typically provided by seasoned leaders who understand the value of multiplying new leaders, you get dinged … sometimes by those who work and/or report to you … and sometimes by yourself. Leaders who have weathered storms know that one of the best things they can do is reach out and prepare the next layer for their upcoming new roles. They do it by example. They do it by mentoring.

As a new leader you may be apprehensive. You want to know:

- Does my team have confidence in my ability to lead them to success?

- Do they respect me?

- Will they listen to me, or will they just ignore me?

- Will they take me seriously?

Notice … I did not say *Will they like me? Can we be friends?* This is not the role of the leader. Sure, they may like you and friendships may develop … but this is not a requirement. Don't get stuck in this lane.

Building Your Support

Stepping into a leadership role as a neophyte can be both challenging, exciting, and scary, all at the same time. If you are a new manager and being promoted from within, you are typically called to manage former friends and colleagues. This being the group from which you came can be problematic and painful. Many of your former colleagues may have been competitors or even enemies. Be Forewarned! Be aware of the barrel of crabs—as one crawls up a bucket side, the others reach up and pull "their colleague" down. Be cautious because anyone of them may be prepared to pull you down when you're trying to grow.

Others may have been your friends, or close acquaintances. The challenge boils down to whether you can get them to view you as a competent leader—their new leader. This can be a struggle for both you and the members of your team.

Boundaries are essential. Learning to separate business from friendship will help you to gain their respect. Don't be surprised to see your former friends and colleagues struggle to see you as their leader.

What to do? You must start out from the beginning and establish credibility with and within your team.

On occasion, there are those who set out on a journey or an endeavor in life and get lucky enough to succeed in their first attempt. Among first time leaders though, this is often an exception to the rule. Maybe there have been a few who were successful and did everything right the very first time they stepped into their new role and have no idea what failure is all about: the exception … not the norm. I know these people exist, and you may even know one of these special people. But I don't know anyone who fits that description—not in my direct experience. They must be the exception to the rule.

You can reach your goals and realize your aspirations much quicker with the help of others.

Working through challenges as a new leader is often fraught with struggles—lots of them. Maintaining an environment of cooperation and inclusion as you work through the transition can feel like a tornado has descended. If not managed properly, it can leave behind plenty of collateral damage.

I've often heard it said that sometimes we win and sometimes we learn. So, accept your missteps for what they are—lack of understanding, honest mistakes, learning moments. Don't be derailed by them. Be agile. Get back on track quickly.

It turns out that the best leaders are those who have had a strong network of people from which to draw for help in making crucial decisions. This network delivers a reality check when a tornado suddenly arrives.

Effective leaders know that wise decisions are not made in isolation. When making decisions, leaders often have a group of trusted advisors to call upon for advice and support. Usually, these advisors speak from experience and may have been through the same trials and difficulties that you find yourself in.

As a new leader, it is important to find those people who can help you, and when you discover them, hang on to them for dear life. You can reach your goals and realize your aspirations much quicker with the help of others.

Recognize that there is an important distinction between *yes* people and those who will tell you the truth. Surrounding yourself with *yes* people is one of the riskiest things you can do. Instead, get started on the right track by hiring trustworthy people who are willing to challenge popular opinion, even yours, and who can think outside of the box. In fact, you may have to drastically change what "the box" looks like.

You will self-sabotage yourself if you surround yourself with only people who think like you. Too much of that type of group think can impede creativity and growth. Diversity of opinion and alternative points of view are important for innovation and progress.

Supporters of you and your vision are realists who nurture, affirm, and support you on your leadership journey but are willing to tell you the truth to keep you from making mistakes that can derail your progress. A supportive person is not just someone who is a tireless advocate for you and your ideas. A supporter doesn't look at you through rose-colored glasses.

Finding a good mentor or an experienced coach can be a valuable asset for any leader. As my now retired friend Myrtle Campbell, revealed to me,

> Being a public school superintendent is enormously broad and complicated; and the politics are personal and multilayered. It can be rewarding, but the decision-making responsibilities can be difficult and taxing. Having a knowledgeable, trusted, and experienced mentor and/or a network of professional women would have been extremely helpful in dealing with the monumental challenges of working with a school board with varied political agendas.
>
> A mentor would have been critical in helping to develop strategies to counteract a board that micromanaged and clearly did not understand its proper role in governance.
>
> If I had had a mentor at my side when I dealt with some of the issues and chaos that landed over the years, I would have had less stress and been more efficient. For myself, and my team, I vowed that I would mentor those who were moving into leadership going forward.

Like Myrtle, I'm sure you've wondered, *Where do you find mentors or supporters?* You might be surprised to know that your most ardent supporters will likely be found in places that you might not normally consider. They might be people from industries or business environments that you have little knowledge about. These advisors can give you a new perspective to contemplate. A close friend, your pastor, or even your physician—any one of them might be able to provide you with great insights.

Seeking diversity and breadth of opinion may be one of your greatest assets as a successful leader. You might consider a FOM group … *Friends of Me* … those who believe in you; come from a diverse background; and have business experience. Think of them as your own private advisory board.

Dealing with Envy and Toxicity

Be aware that, as you move up in the leadership ranks, you will encounter those who are insincere and disingenuous in their support for you. One thing to be careful of on your hunt for supportive people is the trap of toxic supporters and naysayers. You don't want people who bring your mood down with their pessimism, anxiety, and general sense of distrust.

Don't be surprised here … they will pretend they are on your side and stealthily do everything they can to undermine your success. Toxic support comes from those who don't want to see others succeed for fear they will be outshined. They are also individuals who are on the low end of the confidence barometer. How often have you shared a bit of good news with a friend, coworker, or family member only to have them say, "That won't last." Or they may pipe up with something like, "You may have been lucky once, but it will change." If they are really nasty, "You always screw it up in the end, don't you?"

Most relationships can be rewarding at times and rocky at others. Relationships need to be worked on and you must put in the work necessary to sustain and strengthen meaningful personal relationships.

You need to know how to recognize toxic support and keep it from hurting you. Toxic people can be excruciatingly difficult to deal with because of their negative attitudes and their ability to dampen your mood or enthusiasm.

Be polite. Be civil. But don't be stupid.

Therefore, select your supporters carefully. If you do find toxic supporters, don't let them into your inner circle.

Your inner circle should be a place of privilege, reserved only for the select few. *Be polite. Be civil. But don't be stupid.* Keep them at arm's length. Most importantly, remember, everyone is not "friend" material, no matter how much you might want him or her to be.

Building and Multiplying a World-Class Team

Having a cadre of supportive individuals from which you can draw for their expertise and advice is critically important to any leader. But that is only one piece of the puzzle. More importantly, you need a well-trained and highly motivated team to get you over the finish line. You need to be a multiplier.

Of the competencies you should look for in team members, these four rank high in the leadership arsenal. Your team members may already possess them so that you can help them to get better, or you must be able to develop these competencies in each of them.

• **Critical Thinking Ability**

Every good team needs people who can understand the logic between various ideas by clearly and rationally evaluating the information and making a connection between ideas to arrive at the best decision. Some on your team will have lofty ideas and think they have the right answers. But what you need are individuals who can quickly and strategically think through a situation and then act decisively. Leaders are often called

Communication is the single most important skill for excelling as a leader.

upon to make tough decisions. You need people who can make a quick, thoughtful assessment and offer a satisfactory solution.

Meanwhile, it's incumbent upon you as their leader to create an environment that encourages critical thinking, calculated risk taking, and decisive action. Granting autonomy to both the leaders under you and team members can improve morale and strengthen collaboration when they are recognized for their efforts, especially when their efforts lead to a successful outcome.

• **Ability to Create Team Synergy**

Assembling and multiplying a high functioning, world-class organization requires teamwork and commitment —lots of it. Inspiring and motivating employees to put forth their best efforts to achieve the organization's strategic goals should be your end game. Combined with your vision, this only happens when the team gels together and operates in synergy.

Workplace synergy is defined as the collaboration of individual employees who combine their efforts to produce a higher level of efficiency in production and creativity and get better results than they could individually. Synergistic and collaborative teams make for a stronger, more cohesive environment that fosters higher levels of performance and cultivates continuous development and organization sustainability.

When thought, emotion, and action are congruent, connecting goes beyond what is said verbally.

Great leaders understand the value of collaboration. They know synergy is taking place when team members multiply their efforts and results improve exponentially.

- **Ability to Connect with Team Members**

Communication is the single most important skill for excelling as a leader. It is key to building an atmosphere of trust, organization alignment and a culture of high morale. What is said and how it is said sets the tone for any department and an entire organization, especially during times of change and/or crisis.

Leaders spend much of their time communicating with subordinates and other key stakeholders. Your leadership team must be able to articulate your organization's mission, vision, and values with clarity wrapped with passion and purpose. They must be able to connect with others to inspire them, whether in written or verbal communications, one-on-one, or in front of large or small groups. When thought, emotion and action are congruent, connecting goes beyond what is said verbally. Connection occurs when you know, understand, and emote what you want people to feel and internalize. By connecting with others through effective communication, you're able to identify problems sooner, making them easier to solve. When you don't make the connection early on, problems grow.

- **Unrelenting Resilience**

Challenges are imminent. Change and disappointment are always present in the workplace and every successful leader must be able to adapt when they surface. Your ability to conquer challenges and bounce back from failure is what sets you apart. To keep your organization moving in the right direction, you need a team full of resilient individuals. They can help maintain team energy, enthusiasm, and innovation, even in the toughest of times. Those factors will become your secret sauce for sustainability and moving forward.

A resilient team is built on the premise of trust. Newly minted team members may not be comfortable with challenges and change. They may shy away from making decisions or taking a calculated risk for fear of failure and retribution. Whereas seasoned leaders have had more time to develop their skills and dealing with challenges is now second nature to them. They are more secure in their knowledge and more willing to step outside of their comfort zone to test the waters.

Mature leaders invest in their employees through coaching and mentoring. By doing so, they begin the process of multiplying their leaders. They help to build resilience in less experienced leaders by allowing them to make mistakes. When you remove the fear of making mistakes from the equation, you not only show trust in their abilities, but you also give them important opportunities to learn and grow. This is the foundation upon which resilience is built, trial and error. By removing the stress of failure, you inspire them to want more, learn more, do more, and be more.

The wise leader learns quickly: People don't change their life because of what they know; they change their life because of what they feel!

As a leader, you are only as successful as the people you surround yourself with. Remember, over half your time needs to be spent making your team successful. You start by adding competent, trustworthy, and committed leaders to your team. Don't settle for just a warm body, no matter how sparse the field of candidates. Set your bar high. When your team is equipped to withstand the dynamic forces occurring within and outside of the organization, growth and prosperity will inevitably follow.

At the End of the Day, You Make the Difference

You don't have to be a leadership prodigy to lead. You simply need the willingness and determination to do the work necessary to prepare yourself for leadership. Your personality, skill set, and emotional intelligence are the factors that enable you to be successful.

A great leader trusts others as she trusts herself. She believes in her abilities and in the abilities of those in her support group. When the critical moment comes, she will be unafraid to act, knowing that she has considered all the angles, options, and personalities. She can take comfort in the counsel she has sought and in the opinions she has considered. Harvard leadership expert Ron Heifetz sums it up, "The great leader reaches the critical moment when she must *come down off the balcony.*"

If you believe in yourself and your abilities …

If you have done the challenging work of building a strong, resilient team …

If you have crafted a workable plan …

If you have assembled a great go-to group of mentors for challenging times …

… then you are well on your way to becoming a great leader.

Leading and leadership is a long, steep process with no shortcuts. If leadership was easy, there would only be leaders with no followers. It isn't. But there is always room for a new generation of leaders.

Leaders who understand the value of arduous work and the unrelenting pursuit of success are tough, and they expect the best out of their team members. They are driven and they drive their team members to levels of performance that they may not ordinarily strive for on their own. Your individual team members, the team and the organization are much better for it and typically appreciate your efforts.

Leaders are multipliers. Do you have a strategy for multiplying new leaders who want to make a positive, long-term impact in your organization and the communities you serve?

Individual players don't make a great team, no matter how talented they are.

—Dr. Danita Johnson Woods

the **Leader's Checklist**

Great leaders are not born, rather they are forged from the white-hot fires of life experiences. Occasionally, you will get burned, maybe even a little scarred. But if you have the desire, fortitude, and commitment to get back in the game, you will be successful as a leader and you will go on to multiply.

At the end of every day, you make the difference ... always.

7
You Need to Know Your "Why"

And I did not want to be angry for the rest of my life.

Everything in life exists for a reason. Everything that was ever created was created for a reason. *Everything*.

For instance, why does a comb exist? If you know the answer to this question, you then know the comb's purpose.

Without knowing the purpose of a comb, it would become immediately frustrating if you were to dip it into a can of paint and then expect to paint your bedroom walls with it. Expecting a comb to fulfill the purpose of a paint brush makes it look as if the comb is a failure. The comb is not a failure. It's just that by failing to correctly identify its purpose, it feels like a failure. When you understand why the comb exists, you understand its value.

As a leader, it is incredibly important to invest the time and energy into defining your personal *Why*. What is your motivation for doing what you do? What do you believe?

At a recent presentation on leadership, I was asked, "What is your personal goal statement?" Initially, it sounded like a simple question. Yet, it isn't. I have, for a long time, done the type of work that I enjoy. So naturally I thought about what I do for a living—my profession, and immediately related to it as my personal goal—to run a successful health center. But is it?

The more I thought about it, I began to think about whether it is the work I enjoy, or the reason I do it—the *Why I do it.*

Do you know what your *Why* statement is?

The question so intrigued me that it challenged me to come up with a personal goal statement—my **Why statement**—my purpose. It took me a while to fully separate what I do for a living from *why* I do it. But eventually, I landed on my *Why* statement:

> To be a leader who inspires and teaches as many people as possible, for as long as possible, to live their best lives.

This is what I am passionate about more than anything else. It transcends my job and spills over into every other aspect of my life. It is what energizes and excites me.

Do You Know What Your *Why* Statement Is?

Knowing your *Why* will help you to gain a more personal and introspective view of yourself while clarifying your purpose. Once you have gained this personal insight, you are better able to define, articulate, and demonstrate to others who you are and what you are good at. They will in turn identify you as a person who knows who you are and they will know that you are authentic and unapologetic for who you are.

Start with your signature strengths to formulate your *Why.*

As a woman in leadership, one of the best ways there is to conquer your inner critic and to develop self-confidence is to identify and understand your purpose in life—your *Why.* There is nothing more important than knowing your purpose in life. I know this might sound a bit nebulous and maybe even confusing. But, believe me, it becomes much clearer if you first ask yourself the question, *Why do I exist?*

One way to discover your purpose and define your *Why* is to start by identifying your signature strengths. These are unique gifts that we've all been given and it's when you are practicing your signature strengths that you are living with purpose. Different people have different signature strengths like musical talents, compassion, listening, or humor. What are yours? Add them to your list.

> **Your *Why* begins with the things that give you the greatest satisfaction and fulfillment.**

Another way to describe signature strengths is focusing in on what you really enjoy doing, as in identifying the things that give you the greatest satisfaction and fulfillment. Mine are connected: learning something new and using it to develop strengths and talents in others.

Some would define this as what God has created you to do. But here's what I know for sure, as Oprah would say, "Practicing a signature strength minimizes stress, enhances self-esteem and brings a positive feeling into your life."

I also know that when I get to use my signature strengths, my life is more positive, my sense of self is enhanced, and my stress is minimized.

Sometimes when working with women, someone will say, "But Danita, I have no signature strengths."

My response is always "Of course you do. Just pay attention. You usually feel your best when you are using it. You are energized rather than stressed when using your signature strength. And other people usually benefit from the experience."

Passion Fuels Your "Why"

Going to work every day is what we all do to earn a living—to pay our bills. We typically do this out of necessity. Less frequently do we find those who do it because they are passionate about it.

A sense of purpose guides you and instills within you a sense of confidence. It encourages you to venture out of your tiny space—your comfort zone—and explore opportunity. It gives you the room you need to grow and to exercise your talents and abilities.

At one time or another, you have had that gnawing feeling that something was missing in your life. That you were supposed to be doing more and making a difference in the world. You may have been afraid to venture outside of your comfort zone to experience new things that could have been the missing piece you felt. At other times, you are just not sure what you should be doing with your life. You search for that perfect job looking for a perfect fit. You feel empty and lack a clear direction. These are not uncommon feelings, but it can leave you unsure and searching to find that perfect thing—that one thing that resonates with your heart and soul.

The result is you feel disjointed, as if the pieces of the puzzle aren't quite fitting together. It's like putting on your fanciest outfit, going to an elegant event, and feeling uncomfortable all night because you're concerned that your dress is too tight.

The good news is that you're not alone. As you move through your life's journey, you must be open to the fact that one day your purpose will reveal itself to you. If you are always looking, you never fully engage in those things that you are passionate about. You are in a constant state of turmoil because there is so much clutter in your life, and it becomes difficult to see your way clear to doing the things that are most satisfying to you. And so, your purpose often remains elusive.

Don't despair. Very few really know what they want to do with their lives. Often it takes a long time and much trial and error before you find that perfect fit. Many times, it may not be your profession that is the right fit. It may be that your profession only finances, provides the capital for, your *Why*—your passion. Other times the work you do may be the very thing you are passionate about. When this happens, it is a total win.

In leadership, you work hard at your job. But hard work doesn't always yield fulfillment. Throughout your career, you may be on a search for the "right" work. The right work fills a passion, fits your heart, and complements your style.

On occasion, you may run across people who knew what they wanted to do with their lives early on and they go about planning and preparing for the day when they will realize their dreams. That's the exception, not the norm. Instead, most really don't have a clue as to what they were meant to do. They are constantly in search of that one perfect thing that will bring them true happiness and fulfillment. Many times, people may even change their minds several times along the way. I did. But know that when you define your *Why*, you will be well on your way to a passion-driven life.

Belief Inspires Your Why

Tomorrow always brings new opportunities. Leaders who nurture a spirit of possibility toward all aspects of their lives—work, relationships, etc., usually thrive in most of the things they do. Believing in yourself and your abilities is crucial to finding your *Why*.

Be optimistic. Expect the best and always listen to your inner voice. These are the keys to greater confidence and higher self-esteem.

As a child, I grew up with a lot of noise. When you live with five other siblings in a tiny, two-bedroom apartment you don't get much "me" time. I was the fourth child of a very rambunctious bunch.

I was surrounded by laughing, shouting, singing, and arguing voices from the moment I woke up to the moment I fell asleep. Among those voices there were some special ones. My mother's soft voice telling me, "You're so smart, a quick learner, Danita." My younger sister's teasing voice, "So, you think you're Mom's favorite … huh!" And my grandmother's wise voice, "You can be anybody you want to be."

Negative voices are far more powerful than positive ones.

But by far the most dominant voice in our little household was my father's voice—harsh, overbearing and often mean. And his voice was LOUD and had a different message. "You're lazy. You're stupid. You'll never amount to anything." My father's voice overpowered my mother's and my grandmother's voices. It dominated our family and it imprinted itself on my thoughts. My father's voice became the voice in my head. And it became my reality—my truth of who I was, although it was an untruth.

As a child, you grow up doing a lot of listening. Even before you can speak, you are listening to the voices of your parents and picking up information about yourself. "Don't be silly." "Oh, you're so clumsy." "Quiet. You talk too much."

These negative voices aren't always abusive. They're often well-meaning, but they shape the picture you have of yourself and more importantly, they shape your self-talk.

Neuroscientists now believe that habits, behaviors, and personalities are all driven by thoughts. Encouraging a child to think of herself as an achiever, she'll probably become an achiever. Rewarding a child for taking initiative and she'll develop more initiative. But by telling a child that she's naughty or useless or stupid … she will likely become naughtier, more useless, or redefine what stupidity can be.

And to make things worse, their research also suggests that for every negative message a child receives, she needs five positive messages to counterbalance it. Yes, you read that right! You need five positive messages for every negative message you hear. Negative voices are far more powerful than positive ones.

Danita, you're always angry.

It's no wonder my father's voice, the voice that told me I was a nobody, drowned out all the rest.

Like so many girls, I grew up, got pregnant, dropped out of school, and became a single parent. It's not an uncommon story. And it could've been my whole story if it wasn't for one voice that helped to change the course of my life.

At eighteen, I was working in a psychiatric hospital. My daily routine consisted of emptying bedpans, mopping floors, and cleaning up vomit. I wasn't what you'd describe as a "star employee." I was moody, I was difficult to manage, and I was usually late. One day my supervisor snapped at me and I lost my temper. It got ugly. The matter was escalated, as they like to say in management, to her supervisor, Dorothy Peterson, and I thought, "Well, this is it." But instead of firing me, Mrs. Peterson took me into her office and something extraordinary happened.

Now I want you to picture my belligerent eighteen-year-old-self sitting there in Mrs. Peterson's office—all hair and attitude. I'm sure you've met that belligerent eighteen year old before. You might even have BEEN that belligerent eighteen year old. I was not in the mood to apologize. Finally, she broke the standoff. Danita, she said, "What's the matter with you?"

"I'm angry," I shouted at her.

She looked at me and replied, "Danita, you're always angry."

Her voice wasn't critical, it wasn't harsh, but it was truthful. And it was the first voice I'd really heard for a long time. I realized I *WAS always angry*.

- I was angry because I hated my dead-end job.

- I was angry because I had dropped out of school.

- I was angry because I had become a person I didn't want to be.

I'd been listening to the embedded voice of my father all my life and that voice had made me into somebody I was not.

And I did not want to be angry for the rest of my life.

After the meeting with Mrs. Peterson, I decided:

- I was going to go back to school!

- I enrolled in classes and finished my high school exams.

- I started college and went on to eventually finish with a bachelor's degree, two master's degrees, and a PhD.

It wasn't easy. It wasn't always fun. And the voice of my father would often try to resurface and hold me back. But as I worked my way through school, and the small victories became bigger ones, I got better at tuning out that voice and tuning in to the voice of my grandmother. The voice that told me, "Danita, you can be whatever you want to be." Grandma was right … I could.

Eventually, that voice replaced the other voice in my head and my new favorite voice changed who I was. That voice made me believe that I could do anything I set my mind to. Everyone needs a Mrs. Peterson in his or her life to kindle the redirect.

We all have voices in our heads, positive and negative, but it's not always easy to hear the positive ones. One of the most far-reaching issues for women is low self-esteem, lack of confidence and a feeling of being all things to all people except yourself. Your belief in yourself is usually formed by the voices that you listen to. As a woman, you must be more mindful of the voices you listen to. You can be happier, more confident and have a greater sense of purpose by listening more carefully to your inner voice. When you run toward your destiny, you distance yourself from your past and run toward who you want to be.

If you are dealing with the gremlins of negative voices, I've included three simple strategies to help you tune out the noisy external voices and tune in to your quiet internal voice. Be ready to hear the voice that's calling you to your true purpose and answering your *Why*.

Strategy number one: *Surround yourself with positive people.* Tuning out negative external voices starts with taking a hard look at who you are surrounding yourself with. The people you surround yourself with can help you out or hold you back. So, ask yourself this about those close to you:

- Can they be honest without being unkind?

- Can they be right without being righteous?

- Can they disagree without being disagreeable?

- And, most importantly, do they make you feel energized, or do they drain you?

The people who have the most positive influence in your life are the ones who strike a balance between being kind and being candid. This means that they show compassion with encouraging words, they see your potential and assume the best—just like my manager Mrs. Peterson did.

The way you see yourself is just a product of habitual thoughts.

Ideally, you want to spend more time with them, the ones who are nurturing. And stop spending any time with those who drain you—who have toxic elements in their interactions with you.

But you can't always rid yourself of toxic people because—just like in my situation—they may be family members … or spouses … or bosses. So, if you can't get rid of the negative voices in your life, what can you do? You can tune them out and decide not to listen to them. Although you can't always shut up a negative voice, you can make a conscious effort not to listen.

When I was that high school dropout and I decided that I didn't want to be that angry teen any longer, I turned things around and decided to finish high school. Enrolling, I was now older than most in my classes. My classes were during the day, and my mom now watched over my baby when I was in school.

Next on my list was college. One day, as I was standing in line to register at the local university, I heard a voice behind me saying, "What's she doing here? She didn't even graduate from our high school!"

I briefly turned around to see who was talking and I saw the faces of two of the mean girls from my high school. I was mortified. But as I turned my back to them, I quickly decided that I was not going to listen to those negative voices. Instead, I focused my attention on completing the registration process that day, attending classes, and eventually received my next diploma.

Strategy number two: *Tune in to your positive internal voice.* This step can be difficult at first, because sometimes that positive voice has been silenced by louder external voices, just as my grandmother's voice was drowned out when I was a child. But by becoming more conscious of your inner voice, you can start to work on it, and it becomes easier as you become more selective.

Remember that the way you see yourself is just a product of habitual thoughts. Thinking of yourself in a negative way is a habit. You didn't seed it—someone else did. But over time, you have nurtured it. You can break those habitual thought patterns and create new ones by changing the way you talk to yourself. Scientists call this neuroplasticity.

By consciously becoming aware of your negative voice and replacing it with a positive one, you start to create new neural pathways in your brain and change your mind. You have reseeded your habits, the ones that you will nurture. But you must do it regularly and you must keep doing it. You must make a habit of talking to yourself differently.

You've probably heard that it takes 21 days to form a new habit. Unfortunately, that's not always true. The amount of time it takes to modify your behavior can range anywhere from three weeks to several months but think of it like climbing a hill—it starts out steep but gradually levels off. In the beginning, it takes a lot of effort but after a while, you don't even notice that you're doing it.

When negative voices are in play, they hold you back instead of helping you to move forward. These voices can also cause a high level of stress as you doubt your own capabilities. You must take control of the way you talk to yourself before you can take control of your life.

This is what I had to learn to do to get through the many challenges in my life. I had to drown out the loud voice of my father and other detractors, like the mean girls from high school. I had to call upon the positive, encouraging voice of my grandmother.

When you find yourself listening to the negative voice, challenge it and replace it with a positive one. The more positive messages you give yourself, the stronger and more confident you will feel.

This is not the same as "think positive." Telling yourself that you are going to win the lottery every day will not make it happen. Pretending everything is fine when everything is falling apart is not healthy. In fact, being relentlessly positive is called living in La La Land—and that is not healthy.

But replacing habitually negative self-talk with positive self-talk has been proven to lead to better mental and emotional health. It's like circuit training for the brain. Constant repetition makes your mind stronger, more fit and healthier.

Strategy number three. *Listen to your voice.*
Once you've decided to stop listening to those negative external voices and you start to tune in to your own positive inner voice, there's one final voice that you need to start listening to. It's yours. It's the voice of your true purpose. The voice that is calling you to be the person that you are capable of being. It is the voice helping you to tune in to your *Why*.

As a woman, you are sometimes sidetracked from your passion by family obligations, the expectations of others or just the sheer exhaustion of multitasking. You are a mother, a daughter, a wife, and an employee before you are yourself. But the voice of your purpose—your *Why*—is always calling to you and listening to that voice leads to a happier and more fulfilled life. It's never too late to hear it!

I will never forget the day I graduated. It had taken me a few years to get to that place and countless hours of toil. My whole family was there: my children, my mother, sister, grandmother and, yes, even my father. It was a beautiful summer day and as I stood in the gardens of Indiana University in my cap and gown, holding my diploma, I heard my grandmother's voice in my head. *See what I told you, you can be anybody you want to be.*

Yet it was different. Suddenly I realized it wasn't my grandmother's voice anymore … it was mine … and I knew that wherever I was going next, her voice *and mine* would be within me, and it would help me to always believe in myself and find my true purpose in life.

Figure out what your purpose is in life, what you really and truly want to do with your time and your life; then be willing to sacrifice everything and then some to achieve it. If you are not willing to make the sacrifice, then keep searching.

—Quintina Ragnacci

the **Leader's Checklist**

Make yourself a promise to stop listening to the negative voices and tune in to your positive inner voice so that you can hear your true purpose calling and be able to define more clearly your *Why*. This will help you find the right path, wherever you are on life's journey.

- Knowing your *Why* can make all the difference in reaching a happy, thriving, and fulfilling life.

- Knowing your *Why* is critically important for a leader.

If It Doesn't Feel Right, It Probably Isn't

Character is a scarce and priceless virtue.

When things get complicated, how do you respond? Do you become nervous or anxious during the process? Are you able to resist pressure from the naysayers when you know that you are on the right path? Are you able to quickly assess if the situation can wait or is urgent? Are you able to let your brain get in gear before you open your mouth?

Ideally, you can answer "yes" to three of the four questions posed and hopefully "no" to the first one. Yet, there are times when emotions run high, or a crisis could be imminent. Or you are just having an "off" day. Your personal character is what will guide you through your leadership reign.

- Great Leaders don't choose the effortless way out. They know that if something doesn't feel right, it probably isn't. And they know *not to do it*!

- Great leaders don't succumb to the pressure of the moment, the circumstance, or other people.

- Great leaders are persons of unquestionable character and steadfast integrity.
- Great leaders have learned that the intersection between character and integrity is vital because together they are the unyielding foundation upon which great leadership is built.

Just like in a Broadway play, character development is to the stage act as integrity is to a good script. In other words, character is exhibited by your actions while integrity represents unwavering loyalty to a stringent moral or ethical code. Character is a scarce and priceless virtue. Society has produced very few leaders with unshakeable leadership integrity. And many of those who do have a moral compass often veer off course because of their inability to weather challenges that often shake their convictions.

Whether in the White House, on a football field, or in an office, history abounds with leaders who have seen their leadership rule topple because they lacked integrity and they failed to lead according to an ethical set of standards. Typically, when a failure of leadership occurs, it does not occur because a leader lacks the competence or skills to do the job. Rather, it is a result of the leader's inability to establish and sustain credibility and integrity with key people.

No means NO

Years ago, my friend Charlene Harrison decided to run for a city council position. The council was a nine-person body, and since all of the incumbents were up for reelection, she was confident that she could win one of the seats.

Charlene was known and well-liked in her community. She had been a television and radio talk show host. She was well-known for her volunteer service, and she was the community relations director for her employer. Charlene had a stellar reputation for standing up for the average citizen and for always knowing the right thing to do.

Not surprisingly, Charlene won the election handily. In fact, she received the highest vote total of any of the incumbents and of any other person running for a municipal position in that election, including the mayor.

Charlene served out her first four-year term successfully. She decided to run for another term. Again, she experienced a resounding victory. This time, the mayor that she had previously served with lost. A new mayor was elected. This new term would certainly be different than the first.

While the previous mayor had been a relationship builder and was very well-liked by his constituents, it was clear from the beginning that this new mayor was going to be different. Rather than using a collaborative approach, he used his position to strong-arm people to get his way. He used his authority and power to control people and votes. His most trusted inner circle included an array of unscrupulous and ruthless minions, who were clearly motivated by power and the expectation of personal gain.

Two months into her new term, Charlene was approached by one of the mayor's minions. He wanted to let her know that the mayor needed her vote on an important construction project. She knew that the project had a huge and financially bloated budget to the tune of $84 million. Charlene was not comfortable with the project, especially the price tag. So, she told him she could not, in good conscious, vote for the project. The minion was not happy. He left and told her he would talk to her after she had some time to think about it.

Sensing his unhappiness with her, Charlene became increasingly uncomfortable when he called or approached her. She eventually began receiving several offers trying to induce her to change her mind. These included concert tickets, extra money for her district for street repair, etc., and even a very cushy job for her husband that had a great title, lots of money, and little to do for it. When the bribes didn't work, she was threatened with the loss of her job.

So unnerved by all of this, she decided to talk to a trusted friend about what was happening. After telling her the story, the friend noticed how stressed she appeared and realized she was agonizing over what to do. Her

Choosing easy often leads to complications.

friend asked, "If it makes you feel that bad and uncomfortable, why would you even consider it?"

Within a few moments, she immediately felt a sense of relief. That simple question, from a trusted friend, opened her eyes and gave her the push she needed to tell the mayor's mouthpiece a very definitive and loud NO.

The revenge was swift. Within days, she was removed from her position as community relations director with her employer under the pretense of a company reorganization. It just so happened that her boss was a friend and big financial supporter of the new mayor. Charlene was devastated. She valued her position, the work she did, and the prestige it brought her.

But, when she said NO, something happened. By standing up and rejecting the pressures to violate her personal ethical code, she felt total freedom. Charlene declared she would never compromise her values, nor would she allow anyone the space to influence or degrade them. It would have been easy for her to give in and accept the gifts offered her. She hadn't. And she was reminded by her friend that choosing easy often leads to complications.

Charlene wasn't done. She decided to do the challenging work early on to make her life simpler later. Who knew where her verbal NO would take her. She could look at herself in the mirror and be proud of who she was and what she represented —integrity. At the next city council meeting, Charlene went on to vote NO for the project. She used her power to push back on the political pressure and felt liberated for daring to do so.

The project still had more than enough votes to pass. The minion had done his work. It was built and throughout the construction stage it was met with a mixture of fanfare and outright protests depending on which side the constituents were on. Shortly after the stadium

It takes courage to make uncomfortable choices.

opened in a grand fashion, several elected officials, including some of her cocouncil members, plus the mayor's number one minion were indicted for several illegalities including bribery, mail fraud, and embezzlement. Their new home address became Main Street, Jail.

Eventually, the mayor resigned under the auspices of wanting to spend more time with his family. Charlene, because of her character and integrity, escaped the fate of many of her colleagues and was lauded by the investigators for her willingness to withstand the pressures of those who lobbied her to violate her personal code of conduct. To this day, she still enjoys a stellar reputation in her community.

Character and integrity are traits that are developed through challenging work and self-discipline. Many people never make the necessary effort to build these traits into their personal leadership toolbox. These are not tools that most automatically have. They only come with time, effort, determination, consistency in action, and personal accountability. They also come with a lot of mistakes along the way.

Always remember to do what's right, not what feels good. It takes courage to make uncomfortable choices. A difficult decision won't always feel good in the moment. But if you are connected with your values, you will know what to do. Staying in touch with your principles is the best position to take.

Character and integrity are the pillars that anchor your leadership strength. Don't be ruled by your emotions. Your emotions can cloud your judgment—emotions like self-pity, stress, anger, and tiredness. Use your intellect instead—good sound reasoning and judgment. Dignity and ethical behavior will carry you a long way.

Character and integrity refer to the moral and ethical qualities that differentiate an individual, and the personification of these qualities in both word and deed. There isn't a week that goes by where you aren't confronted with demanding situations and decisions—and sometimes, it's daily.

Leadership expert and author John Maxwell wrote,

We have no control over a lot of things in life. We don't get to choose our parents. We don't select the location or circumstances of our birth and upbringing. We don't get to pick our talents or IQ. But we do choose our character.

As a leader of an organization that has had its shares of highs and lows, I've found these seven key insights for building my personal leadership toolbox—use them for yours.

- If you never say no, your yeses become worthless.

- Be willing to walk away from the deal.

- You make better decisions when you are not emotionally attached.

- Don't worry about what others think of you. You will never be able to please everyone.

- You won't always be liked by everyone, but being respected is more important.

- Don't do well what you have no business doing.

- Be comfortable in your skin. It gives you the freedom to act in good conscience.

Because character and integrity are so profoundly connected to organizational success, it greatly impacts relationships, efficiency, and reputation … and YOUR success.

Substance Prevails Over Subterfuge Every Time

Character speaks to the substance—the core—of a person. It is one of the most important qualities a person can possess. When a person has substance, she/he is transparent. As a person who is transparent, you invite trust by showing that you are trustworthy and forthright. Others see you as honest and credible.

People of substance are true to their own values and not pretentious. They don't practice deception or try to manipulate others with lies and half-truths. With people of substance, what you see is what you get. They are authentic, have realistic perceptions of reality, are not phony, manipulative, or judgmental. Their focus is always on personal integrity rather than outward appearances.

On the other hand, those lacking substance are pretentious and may be prone to exaggeration. They will typically make unwarranted or excessive claims about their value or standing. They see themselves as a legend in their own mind. Pretentious people are usually self-absorbed and do not learn from their mistakes. They are usually attention seekers and people pleasers.

Dr. Robert Rohm, personality and assessment expert and author of *Positive Personality Profiles,* reveals,

> Another way of looking at this, which might be a little clearer, is to look at the difference between character and reputation. Character is what you really are when no one is watching. It is the REAL YOU. Reputation is who and what you want others to think you are regardless of what the truth really may be.
>
> When I think of character, my mind often drifts to the 16th President of the United States, Abraham Lincoln. History records him as being a person of character and integrity. He also had a great reputation. But his reputation was built upon his character, not the other way around. When you try to build your character on your reputation, it is only a matter of time until it falls apart.

President Lincoln once said, "Character is like a tree and reputation is like a shadow. The shadow is what we think we are; the tree is the real thing."

Persons of character are persons of substance. They are filled with integrity and are always real, forthright, and honest. Those who are full of pretense rely upon their reputation. They must be incredibly careful that no one finds out what they are really like, otherwise their reputation will reveal that they are not who they claimed to be all along.

In the beginning, Charlene struggled with her conscience. Ultimately, she demonstrated that she is a person with a positive character. She did the right thing because she believed it was the right thing to do. She didn't fall victim to the influence or pressure from the mayor's mouthpiece. She was not concerned with looking good in front of others. Charlene took the action she did because it was important to her to live life according to her own personal values.

Your personality informs your attitudes, beliefs, and behavior. This personality or

Great leaders know that through failure, you build the resilience to recover.

character trifecta can be both good and bad. Just like in a movie, the characters all have character traits. They can be represented by such adjectives as understanding, envious, untrustworthy, tolerant. To be an effective leader, you must draw on your positive character traits that represent your underlying beliefs and values.

The Ten Essential Traits of Good Character in Leadership

1. Adaptive

A leader who is adaptive is flexible and able to meet the challenges of a given situation. As an adaptive leader, you can change to better fit the occasion.

2. Disciplined

A disciplined leader can control emotions, actions, and reactions in most every situation. You train yourself to do things in a controlled and habitual way. You can control your feelings and overcome your weaknesses. And you always exercise appropriate constraint because you know that responding calmly can defuse a situation.

3. Harmonious

A harmonious leader strives to bring balance to a situation and the workplace. You discourage discord and unhealthy disagreement. You consistently take the temperature of the group by assessing their feelings, attitudes, and action, to assure the group remains *harmonious*. You encourage and create a calming environment for your team to function within.

4. Honest

The most respected leader is one who is seen by a team as forthright and trustworthy. Your team members can depend upon you to be honorable and to tell the truth. You are marked by a deep sincerity and integrity.

5. Fearless

Leaders who are fearless have the courage to fail because from failure, they deliberately tackle the challenges and learn from their setbacks. You know that through failure, you build the resilience to recover and can quickly regroup to conquer the impediments. You tolerate risk and uncertainty because you build a tolerance that tests and expands your comfort zone.

6. Logical

Good sound reasoning and judgment are essential qualities for any leader. With your consistency and clarity of thought, you can reason through important decisions, solve problems and create innovative ideas and ways of thinking to get the job done.

7. Mindful

Mindful leaders can be fully present and aware of what is happening in the present moment, what they do, and the time and space in which they move. You are not overwhelmed by current happenings, nor are you overly reactive to things that are going on in the moment. You can project a sense of calm.

8. Purposeful

Consistently showing a sense of determination and resolve is one of the traits that people looking for leadership expect in a great leader. Purposeful people are intentional and have a definite aim. You are tenacious and unwavering in your desire to achieve your purpose.

9. Supportive

A supportive leader speaks with assuring statements. You are a nurturer who knows how to let team members take responsibility for their own actions. You want team members to know that no matter what the current circumstances, you are here to usher them through to a positive outcome. You encourage them to think of what could go right versus the problems they face.

10. Tough

Given the obstacles that leaders are continuously faced with, they must develop a thick skin. A tough leader must make tough decisions, sometimes extraordinarily fast. A tough leader copes with adversity. You set high standards and don't accept excuses. You typically operate in a competitive environment and demand top performance from your team. You are a shrewd navigator and negotiator.

Conformity

There have been times when your character has been put to the test. You tried hard to fit in. You wanted others to see you as a person who has all the right friends and connections; has the right job working at the right company; is attending the most prestigious church; or belongs to the right clubs. You may have sought out others who could give you a leg up by introducing you to opportunities for a better, more enriching life.

Would any of those statements about character parallel something you've done?

I don't know about you, but when I look back over those times, trying to fit in was not always in my best interest. Women leaders spend a great deal of time trying to fit in. We want to be liked and accepted. Peer pressure is as real in our adult lives as it was when we were children and teens.

Even as adults, what you wear, how you speak, your behavior, is always under scrutiny. You are always being judged by one superficial standard or another. As social beings we all want to be accepted. The desire to fit in is natural. You don't want to be considered a misfit or an outsider. So, it often becomes easier to conform to someone else's definition of who you should be and how you should act.

As a leader, this is a common dilemma that you will face at times, and it is especially true for women. The pressure to conform can come from many directions. Too often, you end up conforming to the demands and pressures that are imposed by others and are unrepresentative of how you think, live, and work.

Bringing your authentic self to the workplace is essential for leadership success.

The problem with conformity is that it inhibits your freedom to be your *true self*. Women spend a lot of time consumed with the thoughts of others in terms of their definition of women's roles and responsibilities. You are concerned about how you look, how you talk, what you wear, or how you should behave. You tiptoe around people's feelings because you want everyone to be happy and to like you. You devote so much time and energy to trying to fit in that you are distracted from your own desires and aspirations.

But real success comes from knowing yourself. When you know yourself, you are inspired to stay true to your own core values. By knowing yourself, you enrich the culture of an organization and bring wise and diverse perspective to the workplace. For those aspiring to move up in an organization, your authentic-self enhances your executive presence at work by garnering respect and confidence from others. It contributes to your own self-worth by giving you the freedom to be honest and forthright in your communications.

Bringing your authentic self to the workplace is essential for leadership success. The most important asset you can bring to your leadership is to be yourself. When you are yourself:

- You have consciously made a choice to show up and be real. There is cohesion between how you feel, think, and act.
- You exude confidence and create a reputation that is built on honesty and credibility.
- You garner the respect of others. The culture of the workplace is enhanced by your presence.

The key is to stay true to your values and focus your attention on being a person of substance, character, and integrity. When you make those qualities the focus of your life, advancement, opportunity, and the right people will find you.

Today, it's easy to hear stories of people, politicians, and other celebrities getting caught up in unethical or immoral acts. Unfortunately, it has grown to pandemic proportions. These scoundrels and miscreants garner all the headlines with their inappropriate and sometimes illegal behaviors. Yet, there are far more people in this world who consistently do what is right, no matter who is watching, if anyone, but their stories rarely make the headlines. They are people of character and integrity, doing what's right because it is who they are. They are people of substance and not pretense. And for you, this is the type of leader you want to aspire to be.

Have the courage to always do the right thing and never apologize for it.
—Dr. Danita Johnson Woods

the **Leader's Checklist**

In a positive sense, leaders with character and integrity use their skills to foster supportive and trusting environments to benefit others. These will be the more transformational leaders who will lead their organizations to sustainable success.

Finally, no one knows who you are except you. When you get right down to it, I am certain you are the last person you want to fool!

In Conflict Everyone Can Win ...

How to Bridge Troubled Waters

Most mistakenly believe that disagreement is unhealthy and will create disruption in the organization.

Are you the ram in the room ... or the dove on the perch?

What's more recognizable than the characteristic butting of heads that distinguishes ram behavior from that of other, less aggressive animals? Rams are known to be very hostile. Some people are like rams, as they tend to have an extremely territorial disposition. Sometimes they overstep their boundaries by becoming *control freaks.*

Has someone practiced territorial or boundary behavior in your workplace? And of course, the question needs to be asked: Are you a practitioner or perpetrator of such behavior? When two people are constantly trying to overpower each other, it does not work. Of course, both parties want to win; no one wants to lose. And trying to win every argument is futile.

But by creating an opportunity that turns competition into collaboration, you now have a win-win scenario. That is, you want to win, but you want the other person to win, too! It makes for a more cooperative and happier work environment.

One of the biggest challenges leaders face is managing conflict. Recognizing that conflict is an aspect of the workplace that is inevitable can help you steer your team away from negative, unhealthy interactions and move them toward constructive improvements that can enhance relationships in the workplace. Yet most leaders try their darnest to avoid conflict by tabling hot topics, tiptoeing around issues, and deflecting challenging questions at all costs. They mistakenly believe that disagreement is unhealthy and will create disruption in the organization.

One of the primary areas where conflict occurs is expectations. Expectations might be the most important thing that impacts cordial workplace relations. What are your expectations in your work life?

As a grandparent, I tell my teenage grandson repeatedly, "Javier, I expect you to be more responsible and to get good grades." You know that teenagers are thinking about all kinds of other things. So, you must let them know what is expected of them. Most likely, being responsible and achieving top grades may not rank high on their "what is fun" list.

We all have expectations. Expectations are real. They give you a sense of hope and destiny. You all live with them every day whether you want to or not. For example, you are expected to be at work on time. You are expected to do the work you were hired for. You are expected not to harm coworkers. Expectations can be never-ending.

The Three Rs for Diffusing Conflict

Hurt and fear are primary emotions. Anger is a secondary emotion. Fill a bottle with hurt and fear, ignore the ingredients that you added or chose to ignore, add elements of workplace turmoil that others might be experiencing, and guaranteed, there will be some type of explosion.

If the cycle of conflict is to be broken, one person must be willing to accept responsibility for the disagreement. That person must have an attitude of conciliation, use encouraging words, and show healthy behaviors to diffuse the situation. The three Rs for diffusing conflict are simple: *reflect, respond appropriately* and finally *react*. And if these three steps are thoughtfully and intentionally practiced, they can turn a negative situation into a more positive direction.

It is generally thought that anger may be the primary fuel in conflict because it is the most obvious and easily seen. FEAR and/or HURT are not as easily seen or picked up on by others. But believe it or not, these are typically at the root of the conflict. And because of their invisibility, when the explosion happens, others are caught off guard, or running for cover. Anger is a secondary emotion. When you recognize and acknowledge the fear or hurt that is present, the challenge soon begins to dissipate—just like smoke into the air. *Reflect* and *respond* before you *react* is key.

At the root of nearly all conflict is the desire to *BE RIGHT!*

Seek First to Understand, Then to Be Understood

When dealing with conflict, it is important to know the difference between a *preference* and a *conviction*.

A *preference* is something that you are partial to, either you want to do or something you strongly believe in. With a preference, you are often willing to change your mind, or your point of view given more information, a change in circumstances or change in the situation. In other words, you are **NOT WILLING to die for it!** As Thomas Jefferson once said, *In matters of style, swim with the current.*

In matters of principle, stand like a rock.

On the other hand, a *conviction* is something you want to do or something you believe in so strongly that you are not willing to change your mind or your point of view regardless of the circumstances or situation. **In other words, you ARE WILLING to die for it!** Here, Thomas Jefferson also said, *In matters of principle, stand like a rock.*

- In conflict, the person who can best influence a situation and create harmony usually carries the day. This is most often the more flexible one who demonstrates the most self-control. Conflict can be avoided if the environment can be understood.

You may be right!

- In conflict, you must pick your battles wisely. Harrington Emerson, efficiency engineer, and business theorist, once said, *Methods are many; principles are few. Methods are always changing; principles never do.*

To understand the environment, you must show *deference* to the other person by laying aside your own opinions or desires and giving preference to the other person's point of view when no principle is at stake. Deference simply means showing respect to another person and that person's opinion.

One of the quickest and most effective ways to disarm conflict is to use a key phrase, "You may be right!"

Much of the conflict you experience is related to your own personality style as well as the personality style of others. Stress and confrontation have specific points of origination. The more you understand those points of origin and deal with them correctly, the more effective leader you become!

At the root of nearly all conflict is the desire to **BE RIGHT!** There is nothing wrong with being right. However, there is something wrong with **HAVING** to be right! When you display an attitude of, "Things must be done my way! It's my way or the highway!" you limit your best input and choices. You also create an atmosphere of mistrust.

You can choose to be the one who is willing to become the *change agent* in your world

Meaningful communication is most important to a leader's success.

(your business, your family, and your social circles). All it takes is one slight modification or change of heart. Your attitude becomes, *I don't want to BE RIGHT, I just want to GET this right!* When and if that change occurs, everything else will begin to change and everyone wins!

Unrooting Conflict

The roots of conflict can be for several reasons. Conflict can arise because of:

Miscommunication —Leaders must spend most of their time communicating with subordinates. With good communication, you can solve any problem. When communication is poor, everything is a problem. Bottom line: Meaningful communication is the most important key to a leader's success. To grow as a leader and manager you must learn to be an effective, compelling communicator. Communication is about making a connection with others.

A mature communicator connects by practicing the ability to see and act on behalf of others. They put their ego aside and listen to others because they know that others might hold the key that is needed to solve problems within the organization. The leader values everyone and encourages the input from all team members.

Make sure that you are connecting with others by asking these questions:

1. Do you show that you **CARE** about your team members?

2. Have you created an **OPEN ENVIRONMENT** where questions are welcomed?

3. Do you provide the **HELP** that they seek?

4. Can they **TRUST** you?

What is your purpose for speaking with an individual? Why is it necessary? What is your goal? What do you hope to get out of the communication? Effective communication requires:

- Intentionality

- Effort/energy

- Forethought

Ask yourself these questions. Who am I speaking to? What do I want to say? What do I want the person to do?

Remember that you are not speaking for entertainment purposes.

Misinformation is another way that conflict brews and explodes. Workplace miscommunication refers to misunderstandings that occur when team members don't communicate effectively, and the intended recipient doesn't understand the intent or meaning of the communication.

The transfer of misinformation can have deleterious consequences ranging from dissatisfied employees and high turnover rates to overall poor employee performance.

The need for effective communication is far reaching. It can foster trust with others. It provides clarity and direction, eliminates or reduces problems, and contributes to a positive and productive work environment. These things are essential for a productive, positive workplace with positive employee morale and a healthy bottom line.

Systemic Bias Bias comes in a variety of sizes, shapes, and situations. It is prejudice, unfairness, or bigotry directed by institutions toward persons of oppressed or marginalized groups. It is a form of racism embedded as normal practice within society or an organization.

Does bias affect communication? In one word: yes. Bias that is embedded in the way you do business *affects the way you listen to others*, understand their point of view, empathize, or are motivated to help them. These biases can be seen in the systems or processes that companies engage in including hiring, promotion practices, discipline, and compensation.

These practices often have an intrinsic bend toward producing certain outcomes. Outcomes can be anything from practices that support recruitment, to hiring and promoting from a talent pool that lacks representation from women, people of color, multiple cultures, and generations.

When systemic bias exists, the focus should be on changing the entire social environment, as opposed to changing individual behavior. When you do nothing to change the system, individual behaviors continue to thrive in these unchecked environments. And your position of "not doing anything" means you are doing something: You are condoning the inappropriate behaviors and activities. Is that your intent?

Too many leaders adopt a benign neglect position. Yes, dealing with problems is rarely fun. As a leader, it's part of your job description. If you embrace the benign neglect option, you either hope whatever it is will go away … or disappear. Or, maybe someone else will fix it. It doesn't work that way. It is commonly agreed that diversity can strengthen the workplace. It is also understood that it can make it more difficult to get everyone on the same page. Your priority becomes to actively engage in creating a workplace that respects individual differences and promotes cooperation in the workplace.

You can create a vibrant workplace with a change in how conflict and other elements are dealt with. Start by focusing on these systemic or structural concerns. You then begin to influence the social norms within the organization allowing individual change to occur on a larger group level. A good leader understands that change on a group level leads to improved individual compliance as it relates to socially accepted behaviors in the workplace.

Personality Differences – Everyone has them. They shape how everyone communicates. As a leader, it is expected that you will be able to effectively manage people with different personalities and communication styles in the work environment.

Personality differences play a role in how well you get along with others. This is especially problematic when you expect others to be just like you. Several factors play a role in personality development: backgrounds; where you were born, raised, and lived; who influenced you; and your economic status. These have all played a role in shaping your personality.

From birth, you are wired with certain traits or characteristics. Additionally, you are taught different beliefs and values from those in your sphere of influence. This unique combination of traits is brought to work with you each day, along with your concerns, desires, challenges, and expectations.

The wise leader assists her team members in managing their expectations of the work environment. She recognizes and values the distinct, intrinsic worth of each individual and leverages these abilities for the benefit of the entire organization. Learning to effectively communicate with different personalities allows you to build trust, employee retention, and create a harmonious work environment, thus reducing conflict.

Workstyle Differences – Your workstyle is reflected in the way you function on the job and how you go about your day-to-day tasks. People have their own individual style for maximizing their performance while working. Some work better when they can exercise independence on the job by establishing work priorities and their schedule. Others work better in a group setting. They function better when they can depend on team effort and decision making to get the job done. Some work slower and more methodically. Others complete tasks quickly and move on to the next thing.

Some workplace styles foster greater risk taking, where others might tend to be more cautious. Some styles may lean more toward consensus building, while others might be more inclined to gather the facts independently and then decide as a team.

Because workstyles differ from one employee to the next, conflict can happen at any time. When workstyle conflicts occur, they can derail the progress of the organization. Learning to recognize the diverse workstyles of your team members and assess team members' preferences for contribution will help you accomplish tasks more easily. Recognizing that everyone's workstyle is different and developing strategies to foster team collaboration is the best way to avoid conflicts and to achieve the goals of the organization despite the differences.

Workplace Culture – What types of behavior do the norms of the organization support? Standards, rules of conduct, behavior, attitudes … what? Every workplace has them. Some are buried in "unwritten rules." The old-timers know what they are; the newbies to the organization must figure them out.

Leadership Style – Your leadership style could be the initial source of conflict. While some styles are inspirational, other styles can even be an ignitor of turnover. What all leaders need with their style is vision. It must have a forward movement to it. Now mix in styles that include coaching, servant, autocratic, and laissez-faire. If you are a coaching type of leader, most likely you are supportive and willing to guide your team through change. If you are autocratic, you will push them your way. If you are a laissez-faire leader, there's nothing you don't like about delegating the process to someone else.

The point is ... know what your style is and its pros and cons. Understand that today's leader needs to be adaptable to multiple styles, knowing that one-size-does-not-fit-all. I've used the DISC Personality and Behavior Assessment with my teams to determine how I can be the most effective with them ... and how they can best communicate and work with me. I do it with all new employees plus an annual assessment each year.

Conflict is normal. Don't think it isn't. It is natural and needed. Why? Because when you put the subject on the table and have healthy discussions, even debate, about it, you can hear and see the issue from all sides. Only then can you begin to devise strategies for dealing with the challenge.

Ultimately, conflict brings clarity to issues and helps you and your team define the true challenge. With clarity, you can come together on the best ways to make changes and move forward to help the organization grow. Clarity will reduce stresses that are contributing to the conflict ... whether real or perceived. In fact, when you encourage conflict to come out and then manage it properly, you can promote the organization's long-term success.

Knowing the best ways to manage workplace conflict can enhance group learning and organizational outcomes. It also enables you to limit the negative effects of conflict that may cause dysfunction. Here are a few ways to start diffusing the conflict and to make conflict management easier for all.

Establish rules for dealing with conflict.

- *Let everyone know what conflict is and isn't.*
  Most people avoid conflict in the workplace because they don't know what it really is. Realize that conflict is not about yelling, screaming, cursing, hitting, or demeaning people. That's bullying and something that should never be tolerated.

  Conflict in business should never be personal. Rather, it's about sharing and discussing ideas that might seem unconventional; that might push people into unfamiliar territory; or that might entail reimagining what the business is. True conflict challenges the status quo, which is really *why* people want to avoid it.

- *Promote the idea that conflict is vital to a healthy organization.*

  Superficial harmony stifles creativity and innovation. When people feel afraid to voice a concern or contribute an idea, finding creative solutions to challenges is difficult. On the other hand, when opposing, new, or radical ideas are welcomed and encouraged, people feel comfortable contributing to the group. That's when companies find new ways to do something, new systems to implement, and even new business opportunities.

- *Establish rules for dealing with conflict.*

  If people aren't aware of the ground rules, there's no way they can live or work by them. Therefore, establish your own company's rules for dealing with conflict and make sure everyone knows them. If necessary, post the rules on a conference room wall so they are visible, especially during high stakes or conflict-filled meetings.

- *Focus on one issue at a time.*

  You'll work through the current conflict more effectively if you focus on it and avoid going off on a tangent. Of course, when addressing any challenge, side issues or concerns may come up. While those side issues should be addressed, resist the temptation to tackle everything at once. Leave room at the end of the current meeting to discuss any new issues or agree to reconvene at another time to work out the newly raised challenges.

- *Build consensus to avoid win-lose thinking.*

  Ultimately, some of the ideas discussed will be implemented while others will not. So, it's natural for some people to feel as though they've "lost." Help everyone understand this is not a win-lose situation. End the meeting by reiterating the points made and why certain ideas presented need to be implemented.

  If possible, ask for everyone to volunteer for tasks that need to be done. People buy into innovative ideas more easily if they feel they have a role in the idea's implementation. If you're able to have a discussion where everyone has an opportunity to put their ideas forward and all the options are considered, people will feel that they've been heard, and that alone goes a long way to eliminating win-lose thinking.

Embrace Conflict

No organization can or should want to avoid conflict, as it's through conflict that you get the opportunity to define and deal with difficult issues in a productive way. Therefore, it's important that leaders set the example in terms of handling conflict. By creating a sense of teamwork and an atmosphere where people are free to voice their opinions, you'll get dialogue, questions, and healthy debate on pressing issues. And when managed properly, conflict can lead to group cohesion, personal growth, and long-term success for any organization.

Conflict is where understanding begins.

—Dr. Danita Johnson Woods

the **Leader's Checklist**

Confidence, the practice of communicating clearly and effectively, and the ability to recognize conflict and deal with it are essential skills for all leaders. As well, leaders must understand that gender, culture, and age of each employee will require different management skills and is part of the art of leadership.

The big question for you is: Can you, as a leader, take your ideas, your passions, and work with the contrary forces that life and your workplace throw your way? And can you do it with no excuses ... becoming a "no-excuse" leader?

In bridging conflict, the wise leader knows that she does not know everything and is not always right. Be willing to use phrases like:

I don't know ... when you don't know.

I'm not sure, Let me ask, I'll get help, and *I'll get right back to you.*

I'm sorry ... Why do so few stop and not express regret. It doesn't mean you are weak.

I was wrong ... the ultimate phrase.

Your Presence Can Be a Present

What happens within the first twenty seconds of interaction and/or visible intake? Major assumptions are made about "who" and "what" you are.

Your leadership presence—whether it's in person, out in the public, or over cyber space via a Zoom conference —displays openly who you are. To move into leadership, your intellectual abilities and competencies are needed. But more importantly, your presence is what helps you stand out as a dynamic and influential leader. Perception is essential: How you present yourself and how others initially perceive you accounts for much of your success going forward.

I've often been asked, "Is there such a thing as leadership presence?" My answer is an unequivocal yes! So then, what is leadership presence? How you project and connect with others is a factor. Think of leadership presence as the convergence of charisma, confidence, and decisiveness … what savvy leaders project. It is also the ability to approach any issue with strength. The strength, and yes, presence, which is needed in delivering a critical presentation or managing a hectic situation.

When most people think of presence, they think of a quality that causes others to take notice or marvel at you. *She has such presence.* Some call it magnetism or charisma. It's sort of like stage presence. You walk into a room and immediately people pay attention. They know you are there; that you are "someone," even if they don't know who you are. It is a characteristic that people associate with your ability to command attention, often when you don't utter a word.

When I think of presence, I often think of an aura—an impression or sensation that people experience when they see someone of unmistakable confidence, poise or grace. It's the *Wow Factor* that you exude wherever you happen to be. It is a quality of poise and effectiveness that enables a leader to achieve a close connection with her colleagues and members of her team.

But presence doesn't have to be dramatic. It is often as simple as signaling a strength or social status based on physical attributes such as attractiveness or wealth, or intellectual attributes such as your expertise and sharing it. When you stand tall, don't fidget, look others in the eye when you're speaking to them, this is an expression of leadership presence.

Although initially you may ascribe a certain level of personal presence to people when you first lay eyes on them, once they open their mouth to talk or begin to interact with others, their status may either increase or even diminish in your eyes based on their effectiveness. Data show that what happens within the first twenty seconds of interaction and/or visible intake, major assumptions are made about "who" and "what" you are. That's the presence factor.

In addition, how people communicate, their approach, how they relate to others, how self-controlled and poised they are, even under pressure, are contributory to the presence factor. Even a person's perspective or unique point of view causes people to view him or her in a certain way.

Executive presence is essential for influence. Your skill at taking command of a room; your show of confidence as you assume a leadership role; your ability to communicate clearly and effectively along with not shifting responsibility, plus other abilities are important to developing and exerting your executive presence.

> **It takes focused commitment to become an effective leader.**

Below are nine principles to consider that you can use to define, develop, and use your leadership presence, engage people and strengthen your workplace power.

1. Show up as an authentic person.

Your ease or sense of self-assurance can impact how others view you. Robert Rohm, leadership expert and author of *You've Got Style,* says, "Make people happy you showed up for life, work and new possibilities."

Being in sync with yourself is essential for authenticity. The best communication strategy is when your level of self-control, your attitude, and your outlook, as well as your appearance and expertise are in sync. As a present and authentic leader, can you effectively share your thinking and opinion with assurance and self-control? Being able to strike a balance between talking and listening, so that your communication style is both persuasive and impactful, can make all the difference in the world to your business outcomes.

2. Develop your executive gravitas.

A leader with gravitas is one who is respected, and who others are pleased to follow because they see the leader's contributions as important. As a leader with gravitas, you are viewed as serious and intelligent.

My definition:

Gravitas ... Combining a high level of being serious when appropriate in displaying the courage of your leadership, maintaining composure under stress, and communicating clearly. Others view the leader as someone who is serious and tuned into the level of needs of her organization.

You may not see yourself as particularly convincing or influential. You may not see yourself as wanting to be the center of attention. But gravitas is a skill that can be developed while remaining true to yourself as an individual. As you commit to your personal development and continue to grow, you realize that your authentic self can change. You will begin to enhance your relationships and connections—inside and outside of your work environment.

> **Impactful leaders know the difference between being in control and being controlling.**

Gravitas increases your capacity to persuade others and exert influence in the workplace. When others take notice, your personal stock rises in the organization and often your standing follows. Your superiors and others recognize that through your presence, you are taken seriously and the organization gains.

Gravitas is often displayed by your ability to be emotionally agile. You can navigate your thoughts, feelings, and words with a great deal of adroitness. You can successfully regulate your emotions to appear always in control. As a leader with gravitas, you are adept at cultivating the capacity to stay steady even in the most challenging situations. You know the difference between being in control and being controlling. You practice always being in control, being nonreactionary and nonconfrontational.

How you look, how you speak, and how you act are key characteristics of gravitas. Manfred Kets DeVries, leadership development and organizational change expert, summarizes these factors as the three Cs: Courage, Communication, and Composure. Developing the three Cs of gravitas and increasing your executive presence will be well worth the effort in your leadership journey.

3. Examine your impact.

It takes focused commitment to become an effective leader. Being a leader is far more than being a boss who tells people what to do and how to do it. A skilled leader develops, guides, and motivates her team to achieve goals and to continuously improve the professional skills of each team member.

Have you studied the effect of your leadership on yourself and your team?

- Do you get the best information from your team … not filtered information where you only hear the good? You need to know when hiccups are brewing.

- Are you willing to move away from any biases or preconceived ideas?

- Can you meet people where they are in life and assist them in their efforts to reach higher heights?

Impactful leaders are good at self-evaluation and self-awareness. They can sum up quickly how others are receiving them. Impactful leaders make maximum impact each time they interact with others.

4. Lead and serve at the same time.

A great leader knows the power of servant leadership. Max DePree, former CEO of Herman Miller and the author of *Leadership Is an Art,* had one of the best descriptions of what a leader needs to know.

> The first responsibility of a leader is to *define reality;* the last is to say *thank you.* In between the two, the leader must become a servant and a debtor. That sums up the progress of an artful leader. A friend of mine characterized leaders simply like this: 'Leaders don't inflict pain; they bear pain.'

In other words, a servant leader is willing to get her hands dirty. She will roll her sleeves up and help get the job done. No duties are *beneath* her. She will do whatever it takes to help her team be successful. And she openly acknowledges and thanks her team members.

5. Create magical moments for others.

It only takes a few minutes of kindness and encouragement to create a magical moment in someone else's life. Look deliberately for someone who could use an encouraging word or an act of kindness. Never be too busy, even if it means scheduling time later. There is more joy in giving when you don't expect anything in return.

The pandemic dropped in challenging years for my organization. We made it through with the power of restructuring … staffing, scheduling, and alternative ways to access health needs for our patients and clients.

Our making it through meant for the first time we were going to share it with **The day of the big week was set.** everyone down to the support staff. Not telling them that they had bonuses coming or what it would be or when it would be given was part of the secret.

Bonuses ran from $1,500 to $10,000 based on their position and they were given net after any tax deductions based on their withholding.

The day of the big week was set and the glitch hit. Instead of automatically being deposited into their bank accounts, the payroll company cut checks and delivered them to my CFO. What to do?

It was time to walk the floors. The CFO and I made the rounds, personally delivering the surprise check to each recipient—again thanking each personally for bringing us through these trying times.

Sometimes leaders become so focused on getting the job accomplished that they fail to realize that things could be done more effectively, with more individual or team buy-in, if they would just take the time to show the other person that they really care. It only takes a minute or less on the front-end of a conversation, or on the back end, to be kind and show compassion to the other person involved.

It is often said that *People don't care how much you know until they know how much you care!* That really is true in the **Be slower to speak.** context of building strong relationships. A person who feels that you care, feels understood. If that person feels understood, she feels that you care.

The reaction to my walk-around day with checks was surprise … huge gratefulness … and wonderful hugs. It was a truly magical experience. My employees knew I cared.

6. Connect first, then lead.

Haven't you had moments when the person you were speaking to seemed thoroughly engrossed in the conversation, making you feel like you had her undivided attention? How did that make you feel?

You should always be that person! Start with:

- Focusing through your whole body.

- Practicing the art of listening more and talking less.

- Being quick to tune in and hear the other person.

- Being slower to speak.

- Asking questions rather than making statements.

These techniques leave a person feeling heard, understood, and valued. What better way can there be to connect emotionally with another?

Many make the mistake of starting off a conversation with the business aspect of the moment. This approach leaves the other person feeling slighted, devalued, and more like a task to be completed rather than a person with whom you want to connect. You will find that most people are amazing once you take the time to connect with and get to know them.

7. Hone your positive mental muscle memory.

Leaders often must act in an instant. A seasoned leader can act in the moment without premeditation or forethought. In those moments, you come up with the right thing to say and do. Your experience, training, and intuition will lead you to action. Relying on your mental muscle memory will support your decision making in times where quick thinking and instant decision making must occur.

Muscle memory is when you have repeated an activity so many times that it becomes etched in your memory. You don't have to think about it. You just do it. Mental muscle memory works the same way. Your brain works much like a computer. Decisions that you may need to make, either personal or business, will be made by pulling from the recesses of your mind, your brain's hard drive so to speak, to determine what to do. Your brain will pull from your past experiences

A savvy leader will recognize the emotional hijack that stirs destructive emotions.

and, of course, your comfort level to determine the best course of action.

A word of caution: Emotions may make you respond immediately, without conscious thought. A savvy leader will recognize the emotional *hijack* that stirs destructive emotions, then think about what reactions those emotions provoke. Be careful to emphasize new perspectives on your feelings, not the *impulsive* old thoughts associated with the emotion.

Be aware of your self-defeating destructive mental habits and alter them. So be flexible when responding. When you do, it creates your own magical moment.

8. Too much charisma can be damaging to a leader's effectiveness.

Charisma is an important quality to have as a leader. As a leader, having superb intellect is essential, but having the ability to stand in front of a group of hundreds and influence their thinking is *golden*.

But can too much charisma be harmful to a leader's effective performance? Surprising to many, the answer is yes.

Charismatic leaders can typically be self-confident, have an almost theatrical flair, grandiose thinking, and unwavering audacity. They are often good at stirring up their followers. Although coming up with huge ideas is in their bandwidth … the ability to plan them, create a qualified team to support them and execute them, moves them to a deficit column for any type of long-term leadership. Those who fall into this charismatic leader definition sometimes mistakenly believe that talking and action are synonymous. They are not. Most likely who is talking is narcissistic, egocentric, or displays exaggerative behavior.

Charismatic leaders may delude themselves into thinking they are more effective than they really are. But the perception by their team members may be the opposite. If you think you are overly charismatic as a leader, things you can focus on to make yourself more effective in your leadership role include:

- Self-awareness

- Self-regulation

- Thinking more critically about important issues

- Seeking a leadership coach or mentor

It takes considerable time, effort, and energy to be an effective leader, but it can have a profound influence on everything you do! And remember … either too much or too little charisma can have a negative impact.

9. Start with quiet strength.

Prepare yourself to start with quiet strength. Many leaders become overly anxious before and during speaking. It's not easy to calm your nerves and control your body when anxiety sets in. You may even feel exposed standing in front of an audience, especially when there is no lectern or table to grab a hold of and hide behind.

The key to controlling your jitters is to practice standing still for a few seconds, take control of your breathing and then start to speak. Consider starting with a question. Your listeners now have to think along with you. It may be challenging in the beginning, but over time you will master this technique.

Not only does it have a positive effect on you, but your audience will likely view your positioning as a speaker who has a thoughtful command of her stage presence.

Start your presentation by demonstrating your vocal power. Intentionally speak boldly and with passion. In the beginning you may come across as overly demonstrative. However, the right vocal inflection will reveal itself to you in time. Use eye contact to create an emotional bond with your audience. Use breathing and breath support to add power, confidence, and authority to your voice.

Control your pace. Don't speak too fast … or too slow. When one is nervous, the normal speaking pattern is increased. For women, the voice tends to kick up an octave or two. With speaking too fast, plus moving more in a soprano range … your listeners may reject what your message is about.

Be clear and concise, using the language or jargon that your audience understands. They shouldn't have to feel they need to consult a dictionary to discover what your word or words mean. You command attention when you project your voice and speak with calmness and clarity.

You artfully move from stage presence to executive presence. That's the goal.

Sylvia Ann Hewlett, economist, author of *Executive Presence: The Missing Link Between Merit and Success*, and leadership speaker reveals,

> Executive presence is not about performance. It's not about whether you deliver the goods. It's about what you signal and your preparedness for the next big chance.

Because one believes in oneself, one doesn't try to convince others. Because one is content with oneself, one doesn't need others' approval. Because one accepts oneself, the whole world accepts him or her.

—Lao Tzu

the **Leader's Checklist**

Leadership presence is crucial to your ability to exude confidence, command respect, express credibility, energize and inspire others. Having a commanding presence is only part of the equation. It is also about empowering others. Leadership presence is hard to define. But when you have it, it can't be ignored, and you are well positioned for that next big opportunity.

Leading the Rainbow

I began my journey at Edgewater Health more than 25 years ago. I was the only black president and CEO in the entire community mental health center system of Indiana, where thirty centers existed at that time. Fast forward: Today, I am still the only black female, and one black male has joined me in this community mental health center CEO space in the state … now making it two of us.

Given that historically African American leaders such as Madame C.J. Walker, George Washington Carver, Robert L. Johnson, and Sheila Johnson have contributed greatly to the fight for social, racial, and economic justice, it is obvious that there is still a great deal of work to do before claiming victory on these fronts.

Although racial and gender diversity are not new concepts in the world of work, the unrest and protests in the spring and summer of 2020 placed a spotlight on the inequities that still exist in our society. Over the past few years in my work as a healthcare executive and during the age of the COVID-19 pandemic, the spotlight has been on inequity and disadvantages faced by many persons of color, especially black Americans who try to access healthcare services in the United States. The ongoing challenges that people of color face in the pursuit of equitable healthcare access and treatment as well as in other organizations and institutions continue to present challenges to improving diversity, equity, and inclusion.

No leader in Western society today can deny that demographic shifts are changing who we are as a country.

As a leader, I strive to make a difference for those who are under the Edgewater Health umbrella, as well as those who are in my community. And, as a leader, you should be doing the same for your organization and community.

Because this was such an intensely charged and profound moment in our history, company leaders and CEOs felt compelled to issue statements clarifying their commitment to diversity, equity, and inclusion in the workplace. Many even went to the extent of launching initiatives and programs to address cultural biases and to combat discrimination in their organizations. But they have struggled at building impactful work environments that establish and promote diversity, equity, and inclusion.

At almost every time in the history of the US, Black and Hispanic workers have experienced higher unemployment rates, and have endured slower recovery than their white counterparts during times of economic upheaval. And in times such as these, women lose their jobs at much higher rates than males illustrating that ethnicity is not the only driver of biases and inequities in the work environment.

Peter Drucker, author of *Managing in Turbulent Times,* wrote,

> A time of turbulence is a dangerous time, but its greatest danger is a temptation to deny reality.

No leader in Western society today can deny that demographic shifts are changing who we are as a country. The impact of this growing and everchanging demographic shift is reshaping not only our country, but our institutions and organizations as well.

Historically, the remarkable contributions of people from different races, cultures, genders, talents, skill sets, disabilities, and beliefs coming together have been life-changing. They've delivered innovative ideas, solved problems, created, and executed plans to move companies toward success more effectively and efficiently than anyone had envisioned.

Too often, what those efforts do is create an environment of DOA ... dead on arrival.

Because change is happening so fast, strategies and executable plans to address the diversity, equity, and inclusion are more essential than ever. Not only is it essential, but it must be done.

Diversity, equity, and inclusion are not simply concepts conceived to acknowledge race and gender. Instead, they become a promotion for growth; a way of recognizing different talents, ideas, and perspectives brought by varying backgrounds and cultures that great leaders can harness to create powerfully successful organizations.

Tim Wise is a prominent antiracist educator and writer. In his book, *Dispatches from the Race War*, he examines diversity, equity, and inclusion (DEI) efforts in education, government, and/or corporate settings, and how their efforts either support real change or perpetuate institutional inequity. Wise suggests that much of what gets done under the rubric of DEI doesn't challenge fundamental cultural norms or practices that contribute to inequity. Too often, what those efforts do is create an environment of DOA … dead on arrival, regardless of the good intentions of those charged with implementing them. He warns,

> Until those structural impediments to change are explored and altered, institutions are setting up their DEI officers for failure, letting down their employees, staff and/or students of color, and doing real damage to the cause of justice.

DEI efforts that promote structural changes and challenge institutional norms are what is needed in the workplace and other institutions. The benefits of a robust diversity, equity, and inclusion program are immeasurable and can move real efforts forward. The benefits include:

- Encouraging diverse cultural perspectives that can create a more collaborative environment and encourage acceptance and respect.

- Ability to tap into local market knowledge and expertise to target specific needs of a group or community.

- Better opportunity to identify and address both conscious and unconscious bias through personal and professional growth.

- Increased productivity resulting from the consideration of multiple perspectives and creation of new and innovative ideas to solve problems.

- Increased market share and profitability resulting from offering a broader range of products and services.

- Brand recognition as a great employer with a diverse workplace that is welcoming and tolerant of people from all backgrounds.

Striving to create a diverse workforce and the inclusion of people is not simply a good thing to do. It is something that is needed. And it shows that when we include other voices in all aspects of the organization, such as planning and operations, it becomes a mutually beneficial relationship. It brings a value-based perspective to all discussions and decisions that can boost employee morale and improve the bottom line.

Leaders don't know what they don't know.

Creating a truly diverse, equitable, and inclusive organization is not always easy. Many organizations encounter barriers to developing and implementing DEI strategies that lead to real change. Although many organization leaders understand and appreciate the value of creating a diverse and inclusive work environment, the facts indicate that many diversity programs don't work. Despite the best efforts, failure rates of these programs are quite high.

During challenging times when cultural and racial conflicts tend to bubble to the surface, many leaders enthusiastically seize the opportunity to bring DEI efforts forward, with a goal and an aspiration to promote fast change. But a sustainable

DEI program and culture requires the elevation and advancement of an environment that embraces cultural competency, cultural humility, and cultural enlightenment. These tools can bring about effective, long-term change management that can withstand the pressures of difficult times.

When it comes to understanding and adapting to the needs and desires of those who are underrepresented, leaders don't know what they don't know. Therefore, it becomes imperative that organizations engage in DEI education to improve cultural awareness, and critical thinking. This in turn tends to foster higher degrees of engagement, productivity, and innovation that ultimately improve an organization's financial bottom line.

5 Common Challenges and Opportunities to Improve DEI Efforts

1. Strategic Prioritization

Having a robust DEI (diversity, equity, inclusion) strategy should be an intentional effort on the part of leadership. As a leadership priority, DEI activity should be deliberate and should be used to establish priorities, focus energy and resources, strengthen operations, ensure that all employees are working toward common goals and intended outcomes to create a welcoming and inclusive culture in the workplace. Leadership should set goals and time lines and hold employees accountable.

2. Conscious and Unconscious Resistance to Culture Change

A healthy work environment is about more than procedures, productivity, or personnel. Instead, it's about infusing a culture and inspiring a way of employee engagement that fosters trust and promotes transparency.

Your experiences from the past shape your perceptions and opinions sometimes consciously and sometimes unconsciously. Unconscious biases are referred to as subconscious preferences that impact your thoughts, attitudes, and beliefs. In the workplace, it may affect your decision making as it relates to hiring, discipline, and promotional practices. And it may affect your relationships and how you interact with others.

Negative and deleterious effects of unconscious bias impact individuals and organizations in harmful ways.

Unconscious biases are not illegal. You may be wondering why. It's because they typically don't involve overt or intentional discrimination toward another. However, the negative and deleterious effects of unconscious bias impact individuals and organizations in harmful ways. It is important that as a leader, you develop self-awareness and self-reflection techniques so that you become attuned to your behaviors, attitudes, and feelings that could manifest as discriminatory or biased. Creating personal change through self-awareness can be a first step to creating a cultural transformation in your organization. People are watching your change.

3. Implementation Failures/Resources

Many DEI strategies fail due to poor implementation, little leadership buy-in, failure to understand the value of DEI initiatives, and lack of consistency of effort. The best way to avoid some of these common stumbling blocks is to assess the level of readiness for your efforts before launching any DEI program. You can do this in several ways:

- Survey your employees and gather their feedback regarding their levels of cultural competence.
- Solicit key stakeholder input from clients, referral sources, and payors.
- Develop a budget and resources needed for successful implementation.
- Determine cultural awareness and diversity training needs of leadership.
- Empower leaders to act and make changes in accordance with the program plan.
- Establish metrics for monitoring the efficacy of your DEI program.
- Identify a diversity, equity, and inclusion champion to lead this effort, preferably a C-suite level employee.

By taking these steps ahead of time, you can gather input from a variety of sources who will feel a part of the process and identify areas where change is needed.

4. Global Fit

Some leaders recognize that there are many sectors of the population who feel ostracized—never to be understood or accepted. And there are some leaders blinded to what others feel. There are many groups of people who feel as if they live on the fringes. Several diverse groups represented by

They are doomed to failure.

race, sexual orientation, gender, disability, and more are just a few of the many marginalized populations in our society and workplaces.

To think that they are homogeneous in their beliefs, needs, and concerns would be a mistake. DEI programs that use a one-size-fits-all approach are at high risk. They are doomed to failure. Plus, some individuals may fall into more than one group. For instance, a black person may identify as having a disability or being LGBTQ. Leaders who understand and give voice to the various perspectives and the multifaceted needs of marginalized populations in a cohesive and unified fashion have the best chance of success. Remember, one size never fits all.

5. There is no end point

Building an inclusive culture is never-ending. Sustainable programs are built into the culture of an organization and become part of the DNA as the organization develops and grows. The value and power of diversity is well understood and embraced by successful leaders. The best leaders understand that having the talented people in place who bring diversity of thought, opinion, and perspective to the workplace is invaluable.

Managers and employees are encouraged to support diversity and inclusion efforts in the workplace and hold themselves accountable for clearly articulated and understood workplace standards. These things don't happen overnight. But a sincere and well-planned strategy can build and strengthen diversity, equity, and inclusion efforts well into the future.

A company that creates a culture that engages all employees in their DEI efforts builds employee loyalty and trust. They feel seen, supported and as if their voices matter. The result is employees believe they are part of the meaningful change that is happening.

To Serve Is to Live.

—Frances Hesselebein

the **Leader's Checklist**

As a leader, it is your obligation to learn and implement best practices for getting buy-in at all levels of the organization. This is a crucial component to changing mindsets and developing a world-class team. The benefits and value of this approach are tremendous as it allows leaders to improve the impact that diversity, equity, and inclusion have on team performance.

The Power of Strategic Questions

The best leaders understand conversations are not competitions to be won.

Asking the right questions at the right time can be the cornerstone of great leadership. As a leader, asking the right questions of your leadership team can spark conversations that give you key insights as to how the business is doing and what things you can do to improve operations.

In his book, *Good Leaders Ask Great Questions,* author John Maxwell explores the process of how becoming a successful leader is determined by knowing the right questions to ask of your leadership team and using the information gained in the process to your advantage. It's time for you to start the asking:

- What are the questions leaders should ask themselves?
- What questions should they ask members of their team?

Mike Myatt, author of *The CEO's Survival Manual,* says,

> The best leaders don't engage in monologue: they stimulate conversations. They understand conversations are not competitions to be won, but opportunities to enrich, inspire, challenge, illuminate and learn. So, what makes for great dialogue? Great questions.

Great questions help you to measure the pulse of your organization. Asking thought provoking questions can help to engage your team members' best thinking. It sparks critical thinking, innovation, and collaboration.

13 Essential Questions for Leadership Success

1. Who are you and why do you exist?

The fundamental questions you need to ask are:

- Why is the work you do important?
- What problem does it solve?

Inferior quality easily results in less demand for services and lower productivity.

These questions define your organization's purpose and is the reason the organization exists.

When you can plainly articulate your organization's purpose, your direction and decisions become clear. All organization activity is guided by it. When your overall strategy and resources are guided by your purpose, you are on the path to success.

2. Do you have a growth strategy?

Having a growth strategy for your organization carries with it many benefits. As a strategic initiative, it increases the opportunity for short- and long-term viability. When considering growth, larger organizations have the capacity to realize greater efficiencies from economies of scale. They are also able to weather fluctuations in market conditions. Successful larger organizations enjoy greater profit margins. These organizations are perceived as having greater prestige and power in the economy.

3. Is your leadership team focused on maximizing revenue while maintaining quality?

Quality and maximizing organization revenue are not mutually exclusive. As a leader, you play a significant role in how productivity and quality affect the profitability of an organization. Successful organizations typically have a quality improvement plan that measures outcome. Inferior quality easily results in less demand for services and lower productivity. Greater quality reduces errors, waste of resources, need for do-overs, and encourages better time management. Good control efforts can have a positive impact on revenue and profits.

4. What is your client retention rate?

Retention is important in any business: be it clients … customers … consumers … employees. Retention not only measures the success of the organization and how effective it is at acquiring new customers, but also how successful it is at satisfying existing customers … and at employee retention as well.

Acquisition of new customers and retention of all components—clients, customers, consumers, and employees— increase return on investment (ROI), encourages customer loyalty, and enhances the organization's brand. Many cities identify the best places to work within it … would that be yours?

5. Is your business profitable?

Profitability is the primary goal of all business undertakings. Even as a not-for-profit, profitability is the key to your survival. It still surprises me to think of the many not-for-profit leaders who do not view profitability as important. How could it not be?

Profitability is measured with revenues and expenses. Profits are essential to the organization's survival and long-term growth initiatives. That means that there needs to be excessive revenues over expenses. Excess profits can provide for increased working capital to manage the highs and lows of cash flow throughout the year.

6. What programs are your loss leaders, or simply losers?

Don't be too quick to discontinue programs or services that appear, on the surface, to be losers. Loss leaders are goods or services offered at significant discounts, sometimes below cost, to attract clients and to promote other often more costly goods or services, thereby increasing the bottom line. This is a business practice that typically pays for itself by creating greater volume and often generates goodwill among your clients.

7. Where does your revenue come from, and do you need to diversify your revenue streams for long-term viability?

Revenue is the money received by the organization for doing business. It is the lifeline of the organization. Knowing your revenue sources can give you important insights into the business, such as which programs are profitable and which are not. It can guide you in making decisions about what services to increase and which to cut back on.

8. Do you have consistent positive cash flow?

Being able to finance the many activities of your organization with the incoming revenue and maintain a healthy bottom line can be a challenge. Positive cash flow allows you to pay your expenses on time, pay down your debt, provides capital to reinvest in the organization, return money to shareholders, and helps to safeguard against future financial challenges.

Negative cash flow signals that the organization's liquid assets are decreasing. Having good monthly financial statements is an excellent way to measure cash inflow and outflow to the organization. Having cash available is a crucial requirement for businesses to stay solvent and avoid bankruptcy.

9. Do you have the right pricing strategy?

The method that you use to determine the price of your products or services is your pricing strategy. There are many components that go into establishing price including labor costs, overhead, cost of goods and supplies, market conditions, and ability to pay.

How much a customer is asked to pay is one of the most important ways in which the consumer chooses what products or services to buy and where to buy them. Being competitive in the marketplace is based on your ability to optimize sales and profits. Successful leaders know that the best pricing strategy is one that takes all these things into consideration and then come up with the best price for the products or services offered.

10. How much risk are you willing to take?

Some amount of risk-taking in business is normal. For instance, you are taking a risk when you hire a new employee. And you take a risk when you implement a new product or service.

Risk-taking can yield bold and exciting changes.

Intelligent risk-taking is when you weigh all the benefits and weaknesses of a situation before acting. It is a thoughtful and deliberate weighing of options looking at both the problem and possible solutions. Leaders must have a tolerance for risk. When coupled with an expectation that has been carefully considered, risk-taking can yield bold and exciting changes for your organization.

11. Who are your competitors?

In business, competition is the contest or rivalry between like businesses or comparable products competing in the same industry or field. Savvy leaders know who their competitors are and what they are offering.

Competition, although not always good, is a fact of life in business. It can be healthy in business because it can force you to innovate to stay ahead of the competition. Yet the threat of looming rivals can be a demotivator if not managed properly. The ability to carve out your own distinct niche in business will set you apart from your competitors.

As a successful leader, it is important to understand that competition can be an effective tool for growing and improving your business. Embrace competition. It will force you to look at your business from a different perspective by creating new ideas that help you to stand out in the business world.

12. What is your marketing strategy?

Successful organizations understand the importance of marketing. In past years, marketing has been the first thing to eliminate in challenging economic times. Leaders cannot afford to axe marketing from the continuing success of their business. It is a critical component of an organization's strategy. A good marketing strategy can yield positive benefits by reaching new consumers and creating long-term consumers of your products or services.

A marketing plan that clarifies your organization's brand in its key message, gathers and analyzes data on target audiences, and clearly states the organization's value proposition should be a part of your game plan.

13. Are you getting consistent referrals?

The best marketing always comes from happy clients, customers, consumers, and employees. The power of referrals can never be undervalued or understated. Do not hesitate to ask for them.

A savvy leader wants to be well informed, so she seeks the right information at the right time to make the right decisions.

—Dr. Danita Johnson Woods

the **Leader's Checklist**

By asking the right questions of the right people, you can gain crucial information that will help you to make better decisions as a leader. The right questions can provide clarity and open the dialogue for continued learning and innovation.

13 Final Thoughts: Believe in Yourself

Great leaders are not born. Rather they are forged from the white-hot fires of life experiences.

It's been said that you are born alone, and you die alone. Some may see that as a sad thing. To me, it's joyous, resounding proof that all the power and wisdom needed in this life resides within each of you. Each of you has yourself and that, in a unique and profound way, is more than enough.

I'm not suggesting that you were put on this earth to go it alone. On the contrary, other people are one of the most precious gifts that you are given as a leader and as a human being. People are a tremendous wellspring of love, support, and wise counsel. When I think back about the toughest decisions that I've been faced with, in the end, it all came down to me. You will find that it will often be the same for you.

In the End, Leadership All Comes Down to You

A great leader trusts others as she trusts herself. She believes in her abilities and in the abilities of those in her support group. When the critical moment comes, she will be unafraid to act, knowing that she has considered all the angles and personalities. She can take comfort in the counsel she has sought and in the opinions she has considered. In the words of Harvard leadership expert Ron Heifetz, the great leader reaches the critical moment when she must "come down off the balcony."

If she has done the challenging work of assessing the needs of those she desires to lead, if she has crafted a plan and a fallback plan, if she has sought out a positive group of supporters, and if she ultimately has an unshakable belief in herself, then she is well on her way to becoming a great leader. It is a long, steep process with no shortcuts. If leadership were easy, there would only be leaders with no followers. But there is always room for a new generation of leaders.

Like it or not, every leader must make the call when the occasion arises. Experience indicates that letting others make the big choices for us can be ill-advised to say the least. Of course, most have been there. We've listened to the wrong advice and if we are lucky, we only ended up with a bad haircut. Unfortunately for those who desire to be leaders, the stakes are often much higher.

Certainly, you may agree on important choices with a life partner or family member or friend. That is what they are there for. But when it all comes down to it, your conscience, your experience, and your expertise must be your ultimate guides.

Collectively, they are the sextant that you use to chart your course in a complex world. Don't lose them.

It doesn't matter who you are, where you came from. The ability to triumph begins with you. Always.

—Oprah Winfrey

About the Author

Dr. Danita Johnson Woods is a healthcare industry expert and executive, speaker, and author of *The Women's Little Purple Book for Leadership* and *The Unapologetic Woman*. She is a recognized authority on leadership and organization turnaround. Danita works with leaders, teams, and organizations to help them increase their influence, solve common leadership frustrations, and improve their productivity by understanding and leveraging their own and the strengths of others.

The recipient of numerous awards and honors including the state of Indiana Governor's Distinguished Hoosier Award and an inductee into the Indiana Business and Industry Hall of Fame. She understands the challenges, anxiety, and conflicts business leaders face daily. Under her guidance, leaders acquire the knowledge and skills to lead successfully. And the benefits and rewards can be immeasurable.

A dynamic speaker and trainer, she imparts proven, practical leadership inspiration, with a special focus on issues ranging from personal responsibility to leading with impact and influence.

Hers is an amazing story of transformation, hope, and triumph over difficult odds. Growing up in poverty, she had a baby as an unwed teen, dropped out of high school, and was constantly told she'd never amount to anything. Her success and stature as a proven leader are testimony to her grit and determination.

Danita shares her expertise in leadership and employee engagement through her keynotes, workshops, training, and consulting. Today, she leads with compassion and conviction and with hopes of making a measurable difference in the lives of many.

When not speaking, coaching, or leading her team to success, Danita is an avid fitness enthusiast and award-winning doll artist.

www.DrDanitaJohnsonWoods.com

How to Work with Dr. Danita Johnson Woods

Dr. Danita Johnson Woods speaks, consults and conducts workshops on leadership, women's issues and managing your health for a better life. She is dedicated to helping individuals and organizations function more effectively through better leadership and teamwork.

She is a healthcare industry expert and executive, working with individuals, teams, and organizations to amplify communication, connection, and confidence so that they can make an enduring impact on society and their workplaces. Her personal mission is to "serve as a leader who inspires and teaches as many people as possible for as long as possible to live their best lives." Dr. Danita Johnson Woods is a speaker, consultant, trainer, and author of *The Unapologetic Woman* and now this book … *The Women's Little Purple Book for Leadership*.

Speaking

Discover the leadership style that is most suitable for you. Danita explores the various leadership styles and definitions of leadership, roles, tips, and techniques and when to adapt your style to keep your team motivated and empowered to impact the success of your organization.

Danita helps leaders and teams strengthen behaviors that positively impact their relationships, resilience, and results. With a special focus on women in leadership, she helps participants gain the strategies and skills necessary to become authentic, credible, and confident leaders. As leaders who yearn to be recognized, respected, and rewarded, her sage advice and strategies provide the stimulus to get participants to the next level of leadership distinction.

Audiences walk away energized and excited to claim the lead in their lives and careers. And her speaking topics include:

Her Keynotes include:

Women Leading with Impact:

Amplify Your Standing with Confidence

Do you often wonder why some women thrive professionally and are more easily elevated to C-Suite positions, while others are overlooked for career advancement opportunities? The answer is that women are often less willing to take risks and often lack emotional grit and resilience. If you're not prepared to take a calculated risk on occasion, you will be stalled in your opportunities for career advancement. Gain the skills and comfort to focus more on outcomes and less on the risk. It will give you powerful, practical techniques to reframe uncertainty, welcome healthy conflict, adapt to tough challenges and move out of your comfort zone to embrace new pathways to advancement.

Conquering Change and Chaos with Emotional Grit

Change is certain, whether expected or not. But growth and progress are not. We live in an ever-changing, dynamic and stressful world where adversity is ever-present, and life will inevitably knock you down. Whether in your personal life or professional life, the ability to manage change and maneuver through challenging times involves a set of skills that can be learned. How can you as a leader prepare yourself for the responsibility of leading change? At the end of this presentation, you will leave with the tools to fortify your emotional grit and resilience, conquer challenges, and master change.

The Essence of Presence and Personal Brand: Establish Your Credibility as a Leader

Leadership presence is difficult to define but we all know it when we see it. It is a distinct fusing of personal and interpersonal qualities and skills that sends an emotional signal to others that you have "shown up." Every aspect of your leadership presence, including your physical persona, your speech, your intellect, and your emotional intelligence converge to establish your presence. It is the verbal and nonverbal cues that cause others to step aside, or invite you into conversation, or seek your opinion.

But presence is only a part of the equation. Once people take notice, what sets you apart from others in the room? What is your personal leadership brand?

Your unique brand conveys your identity, your expertise, and your distinctiveness as a leader. A leadership brand lets others know what you value, what you stand for, and tells them you can make a positive difference.

Together, personal leadership presence and having a strong personal brand can elevate your impact and enhance your career.

Everyone Communicates, But Are You Connecting?

Communication is the single most important skill for excelling as a leader. What you say and how you say it sets the tone for your department and your entire organization. Leaders spend most of their time communicating with subordinates and other key stakeholders. So, why not learn to be an effective, compelling communicator?

Communication is a means of connecting with others to inspire them to make a difference. When thought, emotion, and action are congruent, connecting goes beyond what you say, because you are now emoting what people can feel and you are connecting with them more than just verbally. With good communication, you can solve any problem. Without it, everything is a problem. Learn the three most common barriers to finding common ground. Learn how to create clarity with your team and inspire them to act, which in turn should increase their confidence and productivity. Effective communication is always essential to your ability to influence others and produce positive outcomes.

Defeating the Enemy Within: Strategies to Avoid Burnout, Boost Resilience and Accelerate Success

As leaders, a positive mental attitude and a sense of self-worth are essential to success in every aspect of life. Your mental, physical, and social well-being are continually challenged. Learn ten powerful concepts to build resistance and develop a healthy mental, physical, and social wellness balance. Break out of destructive habits that keep you chained to harmful outcomes. Increase your ability to show up as the right person, in the right place, at the right time to further your career aspirations.

You May Have a Seat at the Table, But Do You Have a Voice? Strategies to Maximize Your Influence in the Boardroom— or Any Room

Women's voices, experiences, and perspectives are often over-looked in organizational leadership. What does it take for you to really be heard?

Even when women get a seat at the table, they are often not heard or ignored. Often no space is opened to allow them to contribute to important meetings and discussions. Other times, when men are invited to contribute to the conversation, women are overlooked. Shutting women out in this way demonstrates a narrow-mindedness of thought and lack of appreciation or tolerance for their potentially valuable contributions.

Studies show that having women on a leadership team adds value when their perspectives and skills are added to the leadership equation.

Learn how to speak up with impact and influence and demonstrate why more women in leadership deserve to be at the table and how their contributions can expedite team and organizational success.

Leadership Style—Finding Your Own

When it comes to leadership styles, one style doesn't fit every leader or every organization. There is no all-encompassing approach that can fit every imaginable situation. In fact, successful leaders understand the need to adapt their leadership style to fit various situations, challenges, and barriers. Examining the different styles is a crucial step in honing your own skills and becoming an agile leader who can adapt to any situation with confidence, class and character, and guide your team to achieve amazing results.

Discover the leadership style that is most suitable for you. Explore the various styles and definitions of leadership, roles, tips, and techniques and when to adapt your style to keep your team motivated and empowered to impact the success of your organization.

Consulting

Want to be a better leader? A leadership consultant can help you connect to others with impact so that you comfortably move to the next level.

Danita provides you with knowledge, expertise, and insights needed to select and develop leaders, optimize team effectiveness, organizational culture alignment as well as on boarding.

She helps you to build qualified, competent, knowledgeable, and personal leadership skills and develop others to become skilled leaders who are adept at managing conflict and change.

Workshops for Professional Development and Leadership Training

As a motivated professional, you recognize the importance of mastering relevant competencies. Managing your time, perfecting your communication, honing your emotional intelligence and mitigating conflict are just samples of the crucial abilities that will propel you to becoming a transformational leader.

Danita speaks and conducts workshops on effective leadership, women's issues, and managing your mental, physical, emotional health and well-being to achieve a more balanced and productive life. She is dedicated to helping individuals and organizations function more effectively through better leadership and teamwork.

Danita will customize a workshop or seminar for your team.

Unapologetic Woman Empowerment Retreat

Sometimes you become so focused on the toil of the day-to-day that you lose focus and forget what's important. A wellness and leadership retreat can be just the answer to reorient, reenergize, and renew. This retreat will provide a welcoming, refreshing, and inspiring environment in which to innovate, think, and collaborate with other women. The retreat is a customized, well-curated and thoughtfully planned space of time where women can gather and feel relaxed and supported. It's a space where a community of women can come together and help one another nurture their femininity, celebrate their unique talents, and ultimately leave the retreat feeling empowered, with new insights and renewed passion to address new and old challenges.

DISC Personality & Behavior Assessment

People and relationships are so important in your life. Are you looking for ways to connect better with others? Or are you looking for ways to be a better leader? The basis for healthy communication is understanding others' personality styles. Dr. Danita Johnson Woods is among the best at teaching you how to understand and work with people to build better teams. Her DISC profiles and certification program will immediately give you a vast toolbox that you can use right away.

Would you like to have her share her wisdom and expertise with your organization or group? *Danita would be delighted to participate in your conference or speak to your group. If you want a highly interactive, informative, and fun presentation or workshop, call or email her for availability.*

Visit her website: **DrDanitaJohnsonWoods.com**

Email her at: **DrDanitaJ@gmail.com**

Call for speaker availability: 219 629-0344

Connect with, share, and follow her via social media:

Dr Danita Johnson Woods

Dr Danita Johnson Woods

@ DrDanitaJohnsonWoods, @ TheUnapologeticWoman

Dr Danita Johnson Woods

Acknowledgments

This book is dedicated to all members of Edgewater's leadership team who love to lead but hate all the poop that comes along with it. Remember—we all make mistakes. But if you are daring enough to correct them, wise enough to learn from them, and courageous enough not to give up, you are a leader!

Special thanks go out to the one person who made this book exceedingly more fun to read than it otherwise might have been —Dr. Judith Briles. She took my early, sometimes redundant, and not always coherent draft and helped me shape it into a much better book for your reading pleasure. She also served as my mentor and coach, and for that I will be forever grateful.

Additionally, the world is a better place because of the many people in my life who want to mentor, support, develop, and lead others. Some of the extraordinary leaders that I have come to know, love, and respect are my support team while drafting this book. Each of them contributed to the book's outcome. They are Dr. Sharon Johnson Shirley, Dr. Myrtle Campbell, Dr. Robert Rohm, Tamara Rule, Bridget Cheatham, and Monica Oss. You each share your gifts and take time to mentor current and future leaders. Because of your commitment, aspiring leaders and those who simply want to get better at it will benefit from your wise counsel.

Finally, thanks to Rebecca Finkel for designing the layout and beautiful book cover as well as the cover of my previous book—*The Unapologetic Woman.*

— Dr. Danita Johnson Woods

Dr. Danita Johnson Woods' previous book

Dr. Danita Johnson Woods' next book
It's in the Details:
Small Things That Change Everything
available 2026